Little Pearls of Wisdom...
The Grace Chronicles

TENA L. NANCE (PARKER)

Copyright © 2026 by Tena L. Nance (Parker)

All rights reserved.

No part of this publication may be reproduced, distributed, or transmitted in any form or by any means, including photocopying, recording, or other electronic or mechanical methods, without the prior written permission of the publisher, except in the case of brief quotations embodied in critical reviews and certain other noncommercial uses permitted by copyright law.

ISBN:
Paperback: 978-1-969367-68-7
Hardback: 978-1-969367-69-4
e-Book: 978-1-969367-70-0

Printed in the United States of America

This book is dedicated to women who are determined to evolve into the best version of 'You.' Reach for the hand in front of you as you extend a hand to the woman behind you. Let us not forget to encourage one another. Let us strengthen one another to walk steadfastly in our faith. And let us always wear and treasure our crown of integrity, as we God-vigate our journey in grace...

> All who receive God's abundant grace and are freely put right with Him will rule in life through Jesus Christ...Romans 5:17

Table of Contents

Preface.		i
Introduction		v
1.	You *Are* Your Sister's Keeper...	1
2.	Getting Fired From 'Me' Was The *Best* Thing That Could've Ever Happened...	11
3.	Beep. Beep. Beep. This Is *Only* A Test...	20
4.	A Love Story *Unlike* Any Other...	31
5.	Ready. Set. Go. Wardrobe Change...	43
6.	The Silent Lessons Of A Praying Grandmother...	61
7.	You Can Dress It Up However You Want, Sin Is *Still* Sin...	75
8.	It's Not What You're Called, It's What You *Answer* To...	83
9.	You Have All You Need In *Your* House...	101
10.	God Covers *All* Of Your Short-Comings...	111
11.	Why Doubt? God Is *Always* On It...	121
12.	Just Because You *Can*, Doesn't Mean You *Should*...	134
13.	Out Of The Ashes I Rise...	142
14.	Author's Snippet...	153
15.	Words of Encouragement...	158

Preface

You Have To *Know* What You're Working With...

"And may you have the power to understand, as all God's people should, how wide, how long, how high, and how deep His love is"...Ephesians 3:18

As I chronicle through life, I oftentimes ponder on the depth of God's love, compassion, mercy, and His graciousness for a sinner; such as myself. Then, I am reminded of God's great love for us I am reminded of God's great love for us, found in Ephesians 1:4, "Even before He made the world, God loved us and chose us in Christ to be holy and without fault in His eyes." God is love. And, because He loves us, He has adopted us and given us a second chance through Jesus Christ (Ephesians 1:5). He loves us enough to equip us with what we would need for the journey (Ephesians 1:11). God loves us enough that He gives us the *pro*-vision for *His* vision (1 Peter 1:20). God's love for each of us is unexplainable. God's grace is undeserved. His compassion is relentless. And His forgiveness is immeasurable. God knew the choices we would make. Yet, He provided us an 'out' in Jesus Christ. God pre-made accommodations for us in our wrong choices. In our slip-ups. In our detours. In our mistakes. In our sins. Yes, the *fall* of man came as a result of the disobedience and the yielding to sin in the Garden of Eden. However, God had a plan before sin entered. A plan for the *rise* of man through Jesus Christ. Hallelujah! The *rise* of man because Christ showed that we are stronger than the tactics that the enemy tries to confront us with. The *rise* of man because Christ showed that even when you are, at what feels like your lowest point, the enemy can *still* be defeated. The *rise* of man because Christ showed that the enemy has no game at all. And all he does is try to make you question something you should already know — God is Sovereign. The *rise* of man because through Christ, we are all overcomers. The *rise* of man because through Christ's demonstration, and defeat, of the enemy in the wilderness, God *still* has a plan. A plan of compassion for His people. A plan of succession for those who believe in Him. A plan of victory for those who call on His name. A plan of *reignship* for those who love Him. So, let me leave you with this little PSA: Stop giving the devil credit where credit is not due! He is not a creator of anything. Only God creates. The devil can only *re*-create. Did you catch that? I just dropped a little *pearl* of wisdom. Listen. All the enemy does is try to recreate 'new' presentations of the same 'old' tricks that he used in the past. Meaning, he will present an old situation just with fresh faces, but it is the same old trick. He will present the situation in a new environment, but it is the same old trick. He will dress it up all nice, pretty, and neat, but it is still the same old trick! If you look back over your life, I am hoping that you will agree that the game did not change, just the players. The enemy only has dominance in your life if you allow him to have it. So, do not let him succeed! He has already equipped you with what you need to defeat him, and He has also graced us with little *pearls* of wisdom for the journey.

If you do not remember anything else after closing this book, these three little *pearls* of wisdom were life-changing for me. Once I learned that there are basically three categories in which the enemy attacks you, the rules of the game changed for me. The tricks of the enemy are: 1) Lust of the eye, 2) lust of the flesh, and 3) the pride of life. Psst...If you did not know this already, being prideful is one of those haughty sins that are considered detestable (Proverbs 6:16-19). Selah.

Do not get me wrong, I get confronted and bombarded just like the next person. However, when my mind-set changed, my responses began to change. And, as opposed to reacting and responding out of my flesh, like I am used to doing, and enjoy doing sometimes, I peeped the enemy's lame attacks. And I remember my little *pearls* of wisdom that God has graced me to gather.

Now, just because I just gave you the tea, does

not mean that the enemy is going to start tiptoeing around you. He is actually probably going to kick it up a notch and switch to a different gear; just to tilt your crown. But do not fret. Psst...If you did not already know, God has given us dominion over the enemy (Luke 10:19).

#TeamTimeToGetThisPartyStarted

Introduction

God's Amazing Grace...

And God is able to bless you abundantly, so that in all things at all times, having all that you need, you will abound in every good work...2 Corinthians 9:8

Have you ever felt so low like you just wanted to disappear? And you did not think that anyone would notice? Nothing that you did mattered, and if it did, you did not get the results you expected. Thereby leaving you with empty wells of *un*-fulfillment. You have no real interests or desires. No goals, no plans, no nothing. And, when you look at the reflection staring back at you in the mirror, not only do you not recognize the person, but you are not really liking what you are seeing. You are lost and you do not know how to get back. You are frustrated and seems like you just cannot catch a break. If you have never resided in a place like this, well, let me share my experience with you of when I did. At a certain season of my life, I had reached an all-time low. If I had to sum up that season with two words, I would say I was living '*distract*-fully' and '*un*-purposefully.' I was living *distract*-fully because I was not aware of God's divine plan for my life. Thereby, I was allowing everything around me, and even more so, everything that was within me, to keep my focus distracted. There was like this haze, or fog, which clouded my mind and my judgement; therefore, making it difficult to navigate clearly. I was living aimlessly, and I felt like I was about ready to lose my mind. I was living *un*-purposefully because outside of work, I did not know what God's divine purpose for my life was. Or, if I even had a purpose. I thought maybe I did have a purpose, but I did not know how to tap into it to find out what that purpose was. In time, I became numb and just started letting life pass me by. I was only existing, not living. Taking up space in the atmosphere. I had no motivation. I wanted to give up without even trying. I was mentally and emotionally exhausted and drained. I had no energy. I had no ambition. Want to know what my biggest ambition was every single day? To go home, curl up in my bed, watch tv, and cry through the commercials. That was the highlight of my day. I knew I needed something, but I did not have the strength to go after it and find it. So, I let the depression win. Do you know how I knew I was really in trouble? When those things that used to put a smile on my face, did not. When those things that used to make me laugh, barely made me smirk. When people would share a funny story with me, and my expression did not change. I knew I was in an abyss. I could feel myself spiraling downward. I just did not know how to stop it. I was in the world, but the world could not help me get out of this one. Trust me, I tried numerous 'worldly' things to get over this 'rough' patch, but with no avail. In my transparency, I had gotten so low that I started to make 'death gift bags.' Sounds like an oxymoron, I know. Like I was giving a reward from me dying or something. But just hear me out. These 'death gift bags' were little bags that I had planned to leave for those closest to me. And, in these bags were several contents: 1) I was leaving them a copy of my book (This was my first book; in which I thought was going to be my only book. But it was not. However, in preparing my 'gift bags,' I was instructed, by the Holy Spirit, to expose myself and to share what I had written. This, however, was not a part of any plan that I had because I had no intention of putting myself on display. But I did it anyway. And, to my surprise, I have yet to stop exposing, writing, or sharing). 2) I was leaving hand-written letters to each person, expressing my gratitude, appreciation, and love for how they had impacted my life. And, 3) I was leaving a piece of cremation jewelry. I just wanted them to have a little part of me (i.e., my ashes) with them always wherever the road of life took them. These were my plans. And, I had drawn them out very clearly. And I was also very adamant about following them through. Sidebar: Allow me to touch on a previous statement that I made. A statement that

I ran through but feel the need to park here for a minute. This will be, what I like to call, my first little *pearl* of wisdom. The statement was regarding my admission of exhibiting depression-like symptoms. I believe that God allowed me to experience some of the symptoms that I went through for a reason. Sometimes, when we go through things, at the time, we do not understand why we are going through them. But, when you do go through 'rough' patches in life, it heightens your sensitivity to certain things. Thereby, giving you a little more patience, compassion, empathy, and relatability when you encounter someone else going through what you have already been through. In other words, as opposed to judgment, you know how to extend grace because grace was extended to you. Let me say this. I have never been clinically diagnosed with depression. However, let's just say, I am a little more sensitive whenever the subject arises. And, it is from that experience, that I have become more conscientious and compassionate when the sister beside me is going through her 'rough' patch. If there is one thing I know, it is that grace will cover her the same way that it covered me.

    I do not know why God did not allow that 'rough' season to overtake me. But He did not. Was it hard? Absolutely. Did it feel like I was never going to get through? Every day. But did I make it through?

Yes, ma'am I did; with the help of the Holy Spirit of course! Even at my lowest, and when I felt like I was all alone, God would *still* send me 'reminders' that He had not lost me on His radar. God would *still* send me 'reminders' of His grace. One of the scriptures that I tried, some days harder than others, to stand on was Ephesians 3:20, "Now all glory to God, who is able, through His mighty power at work within us, to accomplish infinitely more than we might ask or think." This entire verse is dynamic, but it was a small little portion that I focused on, "His power at work within me." If His power is at work within me, then I do not have to rely on my own strength. In which I did not have much of. If His power is at work within me, then it did not matter what I was confronted with, God said that I was going to overcome. There is that word — overcome. I did not really catch the magnitude of this word until I was shown a different perspective of it. The Bible calls us *overcome*-ers in Romans 8:37. We did not call ourselves this, this is what God calls us. Just like singers sing, dancers dance, and writers write. If we are *overcome*-ers, we overcome. That is just what we do! If the writer does not have anything to write, how does he know he is able to write? The same way that if we do not have anything to overcome, how will we know that we are able to overcome? God created/built us with the equipment necessary to overcome. He says in 2 Corinthians 4:7,

"But we have this precious treasure in earthen vessels, so that the grandeur and surpassing greatness of the power will be from God, and not from ourselves." The power within us is not from us, but it is God's lending power. Therefore, I had to learn to stop complaining about the challenges and obstacles that came up against me because I have the inherent glory of God on the inside of me to be able to overcome. Do you understand that in the challenges we face, we are giving God the opportunity to showcase His glory that He put on the inside of us? God's inherent glory is in every situation that we need to overcome. Once I realized that overcoming has absolutely nothing to do with me, but it is about God lending me His ability to overcome, how I looked at life and the challenges that it brings, changed. Do you know what it is called when God lends you His ability and power to overcome? It is called grace. I learned this little acronym that reminds me of the *cost* of God's amazing grace:

G: God's
R: Redemption
A: at
C: Christ's
E: Expense

As previously stated, grace is an undeserved gift from God (Romans 5:15). And would you know the purpose of this undeserved grace; since it is neither something we can earn or deserve? Outside of God's love for us, the purpose of God's grace is to expose, or reveal, the inherent glory of God, in order to make the glory of God known. In other words, the purpose of God's grace is so that His glory can be revealed in our lives. This is why grace is so *amazing*. Because it all belongs to God!

If I had to speculate, I believe another reason that 'rough' patch season did not take me out was because of my gift of servitude to others. Being a pharmacist by trade, I took an oath to be a humble servant unto others (i.e., This was an 'innocent' little childhood prayer that I used to pray. Unknowingly, I was unaware that this little prayer would lead me into a profession where my gift would make room for me and bring me before important people; Proverbs 18:16). In my profession, I serve my community, I serve other healthcare professionals, and I serve my patients. My second little *pearl* of wisdom is to not take for granted the positions you are put in. God has placed your there for a reason and a purpose. I am a firm believer that as you are a blessing unto someone else, God will use someone else to be a blessing unto you. Being in a position of servitude like I am, this did an incredible thing for me during that season: It helped to keep my mind off my own troubles, by putting the focus into helping someone else through theirs. Because my mind must always be sound, I was not given as much time, as I would have liked, to wallow in what was not going right in my own life. The more I worked and poured out to others, the less time I had to lie in the bed and cry during commercials. The more I worked and encouraged my patients, the less time I had to reminiscence on what I had lost. The more I worked and showed compassion to my patients, the more time I had to rest, and not worry, during the night. The more I worked and put others' needs before my own, I noticed things around me began to change. Well, it was not so much that things began to change, but it was how I was looking at things that began to change. Little by little, my tears were drying up. Little by little, my joy started to come back. Little by little, I was able to smile back at the reflection staring back at me. It was little moments like these, that I became so humbled. Humbled because I realized that my life does not belong to me. Humbled because no matter how messed up, my own life was, at the time, someone else *still* valued my opinion. Someone else *still* valued my expertise. Someone else *still* needed me. They needed me to be informative. They needed me to be compassionate. They needed me to be understanding. Ironically, they needed me to be their sounding board, their shoulder to lean on, their counselor. They needed me just to be their friend. In this season, not only was I going through my 'rough' patch, but the entire world was too, with the coupling of the pandemic, in which we are slowly easing away from. If you will allow me to be completely transparent, I would like to share some Chris Tucker, Rush Hour, 'G-14' classified information with you—there were times when I would feel like a hypocrite. Here I was, counseling patients about maintaining their overall physical, mental, and emotional health and well-being, during these trying times. And yet, here I was, being reluctant in taking my own advice. In my pharmacy practice, you would call that being a non-compliant patient. But God has a funny way. I believe that because I was showing up every day, sowing my gift, my time, my skills, and my talents into the lives of others, I know God was taking care of me. His mercy was mending my brokenness in the process. His compassion was wiping away my tears when I did not know how or have the words to speak. His love was blanketing me when I felt like no one cared and I was all alone. And His grace was giving me the strength to get up every day to try this thing called 'life' all over again.

As we take this journey, my prayer is that as you become strengthened, reach back, and strengthen the one(s) coming behind you. In some of the most critical points in our life, it has been nothing but God's grace that has allowed us to prevail. It is also because of this grace that we have been privileged to collect some little *pearls* of wisdom along the way. These pearls are not just for us to add to our collection, but they are to be shared. Shared with the next woman, so that she too, can be encouraged to overcome.

The one thing that God asks is that you have faith to believe. So, before we begin this journey of *God*-vigating with grace. Before I offer salvation through Jesus Christ, I would first like to give you a brief definition of the term *God*-vigating, because I use it throughout. If I had to give it a definition, I would explain this term to mean a process of navigating through life, allowing God to be Lord (Master/Guide) over your life. Now, back to something more important — Salvation. I would like to offer salvation through Jesus Christ if you have not already accepted Him. You can say this little prayer: "Jesus, I confess my sins and ask for Your forgiveness. Please come into my heart as my Lord and Savior. Take complete control of my life and help me to walk in Your footsteps daily, by the power of the Holy Spirit. Thank you, Lord, for saving me and for answering my prayer. Amen." Welcome to the family! Now, let the journey of grace begin...

#TeamEagerToShareSomeLittlePearlsOfWisdom

You *Are* Your Sister's Keeper...

So, speak encouraging words to one another. Build up hope so you'll all be together in this, no one left out, no one left behind. I know you're already doing this; just keep on doing it...1 Thessalonians 5:11

    I love spending time in God's Word! For it is in God's Word that I not only learn more about the integrity of God, but I also am learning more about 'Me.' I am learning more about how God sees me and the woman that He says that I am. For the past couple of months, I have committed to a plan of reading the New Testament. And the one thing that I have found is that many of the parables found in the gospels parallel one another; meaning that the same experiences being recorded are being told from the eyes, and the perspectives, of different writers. Also, I notice that as I grow in the things of God, I am becoming increasingly fascinated with how the actual mind works. In simpler terms, I am intrigued by perception and how different people can have different outlooks about the same thing. Another thing that I love is how the Holy Spirit uses such practical illustrations, to offer a different perspective, or insight, that I would have never seen before. So, when I read and meditate on God's Word, as the Holy Spirit begins to unravel the Word even further, I am like Mr. Spock from Star Trek, "All ears!"

As I began my journey of reading the gospels, I came across two parables: each describing different accounts of Jesus' ministry. The parables did not narrate the same story, but the Holy Spirit showed me that they both offered the same underlying revelation. Nobody but the Holy Spirit can give insight like that. And, if you give me an opportunity, I am pretty sure that you will walk away with some little *pearls* of wisdom to use for your own personal journey.

The title of the first parable is about Jesus and The Lost Sheep. The second parable, that I will tell from two separate gospels, is about Jesus' appearance to His disciples, after His resurrection. The first parable of The Lost Sheep can be found in Luke 15:3-8, and it reads, "So Jesus told them this story, 'If a man has a hundred sheep and one of them gets lost, what will he do? Won't he leave the ninety-nine others in the wilderness and go to search for the one that is lost until he finds it? And when he has found it, he will joyfully carry it home on his shoulders.' When he arrives, he will call together his friends and neighbors, saying, 'Rejoice with me because I have found my lost sheep.' In the same way, there is more joy in heaven over one lost sinner who repents and returns to God than over ninety-nine others who are righteous and have not strayed away!" Stick a pin right here because we are going to come back to this.

For the second parable, allow me the opportunity to compare the same parable, written from two different gospel writers — Luke and John. Both parables are recounting the same event — the appearance of Jesus to the disciples post resurrection. However, you will soon see that they record the event from two different perspectives. I cannot wait to share with you what was shown to me. Before I get into these two parables, however, it is important to give you a little background on each of the writers. Let's begin with Luke. Not very much is known about Luke, but we do know a few things: 1) He was a physician by trade (Colossians 4:14), 2) He was a traveling companion of Paul (formerly Saul), 3) Luke also authored the Book of Acts, and 4) Luke's writings were originally written for the Greeks of his time. It is also important to note that Luke is the only Gentile writer of the four gospels, and he was not one of the twelve disciples. Now, scientifically speaking, considering that Luke was a physician, I imagine this is why his writings are so meticulous. Out of the four gospels, Luke's narratives are the most in-depth. Each of the gospels focuses on a singular aspect of Jesus. And Luke focuses on the *man*-ity of Jesus, being the Son of man.

Now as far as the disciple John, he was a fisherman by trade. John, along with his brother James, were two of the first disciples that were chosen by Jesus. These brothers were called the 'Sons of Thunder' because of their impetuous and fearless personalities. John wrote some of the most spiritual books in the Bible, including 1st, 2nd, and 3rd John, and the Book of Revelation. Of the twelve disciples, John was known as, "The disciple whom Jesus loved (John 13:23, John 21:20, and John 21:7)." It is also important to note a few more relevant details about John: 1) John was an eyewitness to the transfiguration of Jesus; along with Peter and James (Matthew 17:1-4), 2) At the cross, Jesus entrusted the care of His mother, Mary, to John (John 19:26), 3) John's writings were originally written for the church at Ephesus, and 4) Whereas Luke focused on Jesus the Son of man, John focused on Jesus being the Son of God. Although Luke and John's accounts are similar, they each add their own unique perspective. It is this difference in uniqueness that I am asking you to embrace. Both gospels work towards the same destination, however, the journey is just a little different. Which brings me to my first little *pearl* of wisdom, "Never be so close-minded that you're not willing to take a new route, to *un*-learn something you think you already know." Now, we can dive in!

Remember, with the second parable, I will be

paralleling it from two separate gospels, Luke, and John, comparing the same event — Jesus' resurrection and appearance to His disciples. In the gospel of Luke, the event recorded focuses more on the disciples' response to Jesus' appearance after His resurrection. While in the gospel of John, John writings focuses more on Jesus' response to the *one* missing disciple. Same event, just viewed and recorded from two different perspectives. The first account is found in Luke 24:36-49 and the second account is found in John 20:19-29. Keep in mind the different characteristics of each writer as he tells his account of this pivotal event. It may not seem like it now, but trust me, the revelation that was imparted to me will all come together nicely!

In John's account of the resurrection, when Jesus appeared to His disciples, there was one disciple missing — Thomas. When Luke recorded this event, however, Thomas' absence was never mentioned. Like he was present. Why is this relevant? When reading John's narrative, you would think that Thomas was the *only* disciple who doubted, but he was not because Luke pointed it out in his account. Thomas was just the only disciple who let his doubt float out of his mouth. The other ten disciples just hid their doubt in their hearts. Yet, Thomas was the only one noted to have been coined with the nickname, 'Doubting Thomas.' In Luke 24:38, as Jesus appeared to the ten disciples, the scripture says, "Jesus asks His disciples, 'Why are you troubled, and why are doubts rising in your hearts?'" How did Jesus know that they were troubled? They had not yet said a word. So, it got me thinking. Which way do you think is better? To show, and speak your doubt, like Thomas did, or to hide it and try to disguise it, like the ten disciples? I do not know if there is a right or wrong answer. But what I can tell you is that the Holy Spirit gave me some insight that I had never contemplated before. When Jesus asked the ten disciples why they doubted, the response Jesus gave them was classic. Jesus' response was remarkably similar to the doubt in which Thomas had verbally expressed when he expressed concern about Jesus' appearance. Watch this. When Thomas was told that Jesus had appeared, he responded to the other disciples in John 20:25, "But he said to them, 'Unless I see the nail marks in His hands and put my finger where the nails were, and put my hand into His side, I will not believe.'" Now, when the disciples doubted in their hearts, check out Jesus' response. Jesus said in Luke 24:39, "Look at My hands. Look at My feet. You can see that it is really Me. Touch Me and make sure that I am not a ghost, because ghosts do not have bodies, as you see that I do." Do you see what Jesus did? This is what the Holy Spirit showed me. The validation, or evidence, that Thomas said he needed to believe, Jesus spoke these same words of affirmation, to ease the *un*-spoken doubt of the disciples that were hiding their doubt. How did Jesus even know that Thomas had spoken doubt? How did Jesus know that the ten disciples had *un*-spoken doubt? Only an Omniscient God knows it all. Psalm 139:4 says, "Even before a word is on my tongue, behold, O Lord, You know it altogether." So, you know if God knows the word before you speak it, you know He knows what is in your heart before you express it. My next little *pearl* of wisdom is, "Do not just be mindful of what you say before you say it, but also remember to examine your heart. From the abundance of what is in your heart, it will eventually come out of your mouth (Matthew 12:34). In that moment, do you realize that Jesus gave one unanimous response that answered everyone's doubt in the room; including the *one* that was not there? Who does that? I know. I know. I know. Who can give that kind of revelation but the Holy Spirit? Jesus dropped the mic on them, and they did not even know it!

Why do think Jesus came back to show Himself to Thomas? Jesus had already shown Himself a few days before, but He showed up, yet *again*, just for Thomas! Has Jesus ever showed up for you, yet again? Would you have shown up, yet again, for someone who once doubted you? Keep that answer to yourself. Smile. Bottom line: Jesus did not have to make a second round just for Thomas. I mean, Thomas had missed his window of opportunity. Thomas was not there, for whatever reason, when Jesus showed up the first time. So, in the natural mind, one could say, "Oh well, so swell! You snooze, you lose! Better luck next time Tommy Boy." That may have been some of our responses, or just mine a long time ago. But not Jesus! The same way Jesus showed up for Thomas, yet again, is the same way that I *know* He has shown up for you. Want to know how I know? Because He has shown up, yet again, for me as well!

Time to unstick the pin. Now, in both parables, The Lost Sheep and Jesus' appearance to His disciples, the one underlying revelation that was shown to me is that one *does* matter. One *does* make a difference. One *does* have value. Jesus came back for the 'one.' The one is 'You.' The one is 'Me.' If you have never been the 'one,' then it will be hard for you to rejoice in this moment. But if you have ever felt lost, abandoned, felt like you have been thrown away, betrayed, isolated, damaged, broken, neglected, rejected, or even excluded, then we are on the same page. My own personal testimony is that I have been that 'one!' I was that 'one,' God did not forget about. I was that 'one,' God remembered. I am that 'one,' God loves. Not because I deserved it, but because God is faithful. And, because His grace is sufficient to cover all!

Do you understand just how much you are loved for Jesus to leave the popular? To leave the familiar?

To leave the comfortable? To leave the herd? To leave the 'clique?' To leave the multitude just to go after the 'one?' You are the 'one.' I am the 'one' whom God calls His perfect masterpiece (Ephesians 2:10)! His perfect masterpiece, even when I knew better, but did not always do better. Jesus *still* came back for me. His perfect masterpiece, even when I knew that I should not have been doing what I got caught doing, Jesus *still* came back for me. And, because I have been that 'one,' this lets me know that even those with good intentions can *still* make bad choices. This lets me know that even those that try to walk and live by faith can *still* waiver at times. This lets me know that even in our moments of vulnerability and uncertainty, God *still* has a plan. Talk about God's love. Talk about God's faithfulness. Talk about God's forgiveness. Talk about God's mercy. Talk about God's grace. All of that was my next little *pearl* of wisdom. Drop the mic!

There are so many little *pearls* of wisdom within these two parables. If I had to just draw out a few, I would offer you this: "Be careful of people who try to stick labels on you. Labels that make you feel embarrassed, ashamed, or like an outcast for how you may have responded. Trust me, they are no better than you. If the truth be told, the only reason folks try and make you feel inferior, is because some of the things that they have done, have not been exposed yet. Another little *pearl* of wisdom is to not allow people to single you out for something we are all guilty of — sin. For the Bible says in Romans 3:23-24, "For we all sin and fall short of the glory of God, and all are justified freely by His grace through the redemption that came by Jesus Christ." None of us are exempt, but we have been justified by grace. So, why not share it? Which leads me to my last little *pearl* of wisdom, "Give the same level of grace that you received while you were going through your *mess,* to the next person." We are all, to some degree, *transformers*; meaning that we have not always been the women that we present ourselves to be as now. I have been transformed and it was only by the grace of God that I am standing here today. So, be mindful, and balanced, that you are not extending more judgment to your sister-in-Christ, than you are extending grace.

#TeamJesusWillComeBackForOne

2

Getting Fired From 'Me' Was The *Best* Thing That Could've Ever Happened...

But my life is worth nothing to me unless I use it for finishing the work assigned me by the Lord Jesus — the work of telling others the Good News about the wonderful grace of God...Acts 20:24

I consider myself a glass half-full kind of girl. Meaning, as opposed to looking at what I do not have, I try to focus on what I do have and make the best out of that. The best way that I have found to try and keep my glass half-full, with an upbeat attitude, is humor. If I had to toot my own horn, I would have to say that I have a one-of-a-kind, quick-witted sense of humor. So, it did not come as much of a surprise to me whenever God uses this route to speak. However, in this instance, I was not laughing too much because with the illustration He used, He shut me down and 'out-humored' me. Sounds a little crazy, I know. But if you will allow me to paint this picture for you regarding this 'out-humoring' I am talking about, I am hoping that you will understand. I am also hoping that you will not only be able to appreciate the illustration, but that you will receive the message all the greater. I only ask that you stay open-minded.

In this 'out-humoring' session, I felt like I had a 'Girl, enough is enough' moment with God. If you will allow me, I would love to share with you, my rendition, of this life-changing crossroads. Again, the presentation may be humorous, but do not miss the overall message — God will use whatever He needs to use, to get a message to you, and you alone. Not no one else. So, when He speaks to you, this is your FedEx package to open, no one else's. And, God does not have to speak to you the same way that He speaks to the next person. We are each His authentic original and how He speaks to us is authentically original as well. So, do not ever compare yourself, in this way, to no one else. Just embrace how He speaks to you! Did you catch that? My first little *pearl* of wisdom.

One of my favorite comedians to watch is Steve Harvey. I have watched his comedy for years; however, this one routine that he did just kept ringing in my spirit. I was not thinking about it. I did not even remember all the details about it. But I knew it was significant and that it meant something significant for me. So, I revisited it. In this routine, Steve was talking about a time when he had gotten laid off from his job in corporate America. What was odd about this

Getting Fired From 'Me' Was The Best Thing That Could've Ever Happened...

routine, however, was that it was not Steve performing it. His character had been replaced by someone else. And, that someone else was 'Me.' This snippet, that I was watching from the outside, was about me, my life, and the season of 'dryness' into which I had sunk. In this 'Girl, enough is enough' moment that I had, not only did I get 'called to the carpet,' but God put His foot down. Again, I just ask that you keep an open mind with this colorful demonstration. I am trying to put you in the room with me when all this went down. I want you to feel like you were a fly on the wall watching and listening to this life-changing event, starring yours truly. All right. Ready. Set. Go.

There is no way you would be able to appreciate what I went through if you do not know what Steve went through first. So, here is how it all went down for Steve. Steve had gotten called into his boss's office, during a time when the company was down-sizing. Folks were getting laid off left and right. But he never, in a million years, thought that he would be included in this number. Well, disbelief was about to meet reality. There was a 'shift' taking place in the atmosphere that Steve did not know anything about. A 'shift' that would ultimately thrust him into his destiny. Shortly after arriving to work, Steve was told that the boss wanted to see him. Anxiety begins to build up. You cannot begin to imagine the thoughts that were probably running through his mind. Not to mention, I am sure it was like walking the 'Green Mile' just to get to his boss's office. Once he arrived in the office and sat down in the chair, the butterflies in his stomach were probably about ready to fly out of his mouth. Felt like his heartbeat was going to explode in his chest. But he just sat there waiting for this unexpected, but anticipatory, news. And here comes the 'big' news. Before his boss could let all words travel out of his mouth, all the anxiety that had been trapped inside of Steve, spontaneously combusted! And, wherever it landed, it landed. Yes, Steve was told that he was being let go. No matter the tactics his boss tried to use to pacify the situation, and calm him down, it did not work. In that moment, I can only imagine how hard it was for Steve to even process what was going on. And plus, he was not ready to accept that news either. No matter how many times Steve may have rehearsed this possibility in his mind, the mere fact that it was *actually* happening, was too much to digest in that moment. And, as you would have it, the inevitable happened. In the process of all this going on, security was called. Steve was losing it. He was already at '10,' so why stop now? If he had to go, then he was going out with a bang. Security was already headed upstairs, so why not give them a reason, and an incentive, to earn their pay *that* day? How much worse could the day get?

While we are going through some of the most difficult seasons of our life, it is sometimes hard to

Getting Fired From 'Me' Was The Best Thing That Could've Ever Happened...

see God's hand of grace moving within the storm. However, God is so strategic. And believe me when I tell you, that amid what looks like trouble, that is where your treasure lies. I do not know what plans God has for someone else. But I wonder where Steve Harvey would be now if he had not have gotten fired? Would he have the *God*-success, and not just the *good*-success, that he has so abundantly embraced today? Would he be the mentor to other young Black men like he is today? Would he be walking in the assignment that God has called him to? Would he have had the time, or the resources, to touch as many lives as he has today, spreading the Good News of God's gospel? I do not have the answers, but what I do know is that we all must meet at that crossroads one day. That crossroads where destiny and purpose collide with God's will. And, how you walk away from that collision will forever direct the trajectory of your path. Did Steve want to get fired; I am sure he did not. Who does? But did his firing propel him into his destiny? I believe it did. When trying to find the treasure in your trouble, you must know and believe that God's plan always supersedes *anything* we may have in mind. Isaiah 55:8 says, "For My thoughts are not your thoughts, neither are your ways My ways," declares the Lord. So, my second little *pearl* of wisdom is to simply trust God. Through the ups and downs, trust God. Through the uncertainty and doubt, trust

God. Through the winds and the storm of life, trust God. Through the separation or divorce, trust God. Through the eviction or the repossession, trust God. Through the addiction or the homelessness, trust God. You must know and believe that it does not matter what the enemy tries to use against you to hold you down, God says that He could use even 'that' for good (Genesis 50:20)!

    Now, when I had my 'calling to the carpet' moment, or termination day, it was so unexpected for me. I am telling you I was blind-sided. If I had known that I was going to get fired 'that' day, I would not have shown up. I would have called in or played sick or something. Unbeknownst to me, I showed up anyway. However, soon after I had clocked in, I was called into the Boss's office. Psst...In my instance, here the Boss is God. Let's continue. And my 'calling to the carpet' moment was underway. The ball had begun rolling and little did I know, everything was about to change. Before my Boss could even begin speaking, I began pleading for my job. I even suggested that I would take a pay-cut. I offered to come in early and stay late. I would work through lunch, do extra work; just anything to be able to continue with the routine that had become my norm. However, no matter how much I was trying to explain to my Boss, the words were just of null effect. Then, something else happened that I did not think was imaginable. Picture this. Amid me

Getting Fired From 'Me' Was The Best Thing That Could've Ever Happened...

'getting fired,' and trying to convince my Boss to give me another chance, He shut me down. It was like God swiped everything that was on His desk, onto the floor. Almost like He was saying, "Stop talking and listen. Enough is enough." Then He said something that would forever change my life, not in that moment of course. He told me *why* I was getting fired. He told me that I was not getting 'fired' from His company (i.e., His Kingdom), but that I was getting fired from 'Me.' From 'Me?' How do I get *fired* from myself? Almost like how I described earlier of how, at a certain point in my life, I just wanted to disappear. Oh, what a tangled web I weaved. Well, as God continued talking, He began to explain how getting 'fired' from myself involved a few things. I was getting fired from my 'old' job and how I used to do things. I was getting fired from my 'old' way of thinking. I was getting fired from my 'old' mind-set believing that I could continue doing things my way and not considering His ways. I was getting fired from my 'old' habits and my 'old' patterns that were not edifying to God, His ways, or His plan and purpose for my life. I was literally getting kicked out of being the 'old' Me! Yikes. In my bafflement of listening to all of this, my Boss tried to pacify me, just like Steve's boss did. My Boss told me, "I am going to give you a second chance. I know you do not understand it now. But you will thank Me later." I said, "Really? Me losing everything? Me not knowing what would be in store for me next? Me living my life in uncertainty? Me having to commit and trust something bigger than myself? Me having to become a dependent rather than a provider? None of these roles were roles that I was comfortable playing. But God has a way of being *very* convincing and persuasive. And, sooner than later, the words God spoke began manifesting in my life. God firing me from 'Me' was the *best* thing that could have ever happened to me that day. I did not know it then, but that 'firing' gave me a second chance to become a better version of me.

The times when I get 'fired' or 'called to the carpet,' have so impacted my life. The times when I get 'called to the carpet' reminds me just how much God loves me; for He chastises those whom He loves (Hebrews 12:6). The times when I get 'called to the carpet' humbles me because God only lets me go so far before I forfeit my destiny and my purpose in Him. The times when I get 'called to the carpet' have inspired me to live a life of transparency because it is in those moments of graceful breaking, that I know I am being given a second chance(s) (echoed). Not because I deserve it, but because God is so *full* of grace. So yes, getting 'fired' from the old 'Me' has been nothing but a life-changing experience for the better.

What felt like one of the worst days of my life, ended up being so life-changing. Do you know what? Even in my 'firing,' I must admit, outside of the desk

Getting Fired From 'Me' Was The Best Thing That Could've Ever Happened...

swiping, of course, God was merciful and graceful with me, and to me. I owe Him everything for being a Boss of second chances. Well, I have been transitioning for a while now into my new position and I feel a little more confident in saying that my job description, performance, and purpose has drastically changed. I am a laborer in God's vineyard. I work on assignment, I do not have to punch any timeclock, and the benefits package is out of this world; literally. Me getting 'fired' from that old version of myself opened a door that I had no idea I could even walk through. I dare you. Will you allow yourself to get 'fired' from 'You,' for God's glory?

My life has not been perfect, but I serve a perfect God. As I *God*-vigate my journey, the last little *pearl* of wisdom that I would like to leave with you is to not be intimidated by the 'calling to the carpet' moments in your life. These are the moments that can change the trajectory of your life. In order for the oil to flow, the olive has to be squeezed. In order for the wine to be produced, the grapes have to be crushed. In the same way, in order for the best version of you to be manifested, you will be uncomfortable. But just know that God's discipline does *not* outweigh His love. Can we walk this journey together in grace?

#TeamTheGraceChronicles

3

Beep. Beep. Beep. This Is *Only* A Test...

But the Lord said to Samuel, "Do not look at his appearance or at the height of his stature, because I have rejected him. For the Lord sees not as man sees; for man looksat the outward appearance, but the Lord looks at the heart" ...1 Samuel 16:7

Have you ever read the story of Hannah in the Bible? I would like to share Hannah's story with you. But my prayer is that you locate yourself and your own situation through the lens of Hannah. Not necessarily through the lens of her pain and despair, but through the lens of her triumph. All for the glory of God. Hannah was one of the two wives of a man named Elkanah. His other wife was named Peninnah. Because Peninnah had children and Hannah did not, she had a boastfulness about her as you will see later. One of the things that I found so powerful in Hannah's story, is that the scripture says that it was the Lord who had closed her womb (1 Samuel 1:6). Here is my first little *pearl* of wisdom, "No matter how the circumstances look, always remember that God has

Beep. Beep. Beep. This Is Only A Test...

a plan. He has not forgotten about you. Trust His timing because He knows what He is doing. He is able to resurrect whatever is barren in your life." Now, getting back to these two women. Peninnah felt like she had the upper hand because she had what Hannah could not have or did not yet have. So, she would taunt Hannah and make her feel like less of a woman and definitely like less of a wife. I do not know if you have ever felt insufficient as a wife, a mother, or even as a woman, but I sure have. But God. He is able to use your deepest and innermost insecurities as His platform for His glory. I know this because God used my scars, my wounds, my vulnerabilities, and those areas of my life that were barren, all for His good. I will continue to Hannah's prayer shortly. However, I felt it necessary to offer you another little *pearl* of wisdom right here, "Be careful of people who try to use something against you, that they may have, and that they know you want. You are giving them more power and leverage than what they deserve." I say that because Peninnah believed that she had more leverage than what she had. True, she may have had the children that Hannah did not yet have, but Hannah turned out to be the real one with the leverage. Because Hannah had something more powerful, and more spiritual, than all that Peninnah possessed. Hannah had prayer. And prayer became her weapon. A weapon fiercer than anything Peninnah thought that she may have had. Prayer *can* change things. Prayer *can* change circumstances. Prayer *can* make blind eyes see. Prayer *can* make lame legs walk. Prayer *can* make deaf ears hear. Prayer *can* make you first, when all the circumstances around you say that you should be last. Prayer *can* part the Jordan River so you can safely cross on dry land. Prayer *can* cast mountains that try to block and impede you, into the sea. Prayer *can* bring life where there was once death. Prayer was Hannah's weapon, and you have to know that it is also yours as well. From Hannah's mouth to God's ears. When was the last time you tickled God's ears with your prayers? When was the last time God smelled the sweet aroma of your sacrificial prayer? No need to disclose. You just know now what you need to do. Now, back to our regularly scheduled program.

What the enemy tried to use against me as a setback, God used it for my set-up. Allow me to introduce you to Hannah's great set-up. It is found in 1 Samuel 1:10-18, "In her deep anguish, Hannah prayed to the Lord, weeping bitterly. And she made a vow, saying, 'Lord Almighty, if You will only look on your servant's misery and remember me, and not forget your servant but give her a son, then I will give him to the Lord for all the days of his life, and no razor will ever be used on his head.'" As she kept on praying to the Lord, Eli, the priest, observed her mouth. Hannah was praying in her heart, and her lips were moving but her voice

Beep. Beep. Beep. This Is Only A Test...

was not heard. Eli thought she was drunk and said to her, "How long are you going to stay drunk? Put away your wine." "Not so, my lord," Hannah replied, "I am a woman who is deeply troubled. I have not been drinking wine or beer; I was pouring out my soul to the Lord. Do not take your servant for a wicked woman; I have been praying here out of my great anguish and grief." Eli answered, "Go in peace, and may the God of Israel grant you what you have asked of Him." There were so many little *pearls* of wisdom all throughout this story. But I do not want you to miss this one. God used Hannah to birth a *first*! I believe that because of Hannah's heart, her prayer, and the covenant that she made with God, she became a first. God took Hannah from the background to the forefront, and when God opened Hannah's womb, she *first* became pregnant with a son. And, with her *first* child, she became the *first* mother of the *first* prophet to the Israelite nation. Hannah had no idea that God would put her in the lineage of *firsts*. From the tail to the head, overnight. You cannot beat God's strategy, even if you try!

The scripture did not say it, but Hannah was a great woman of integrity. And, because of her relationship with God and how she honored Him, He honored her. There were too many instances in which Hannah's integrity was compromised and tested. Yet, she availed. For starters, I do not know anyone that would not have tried to shut Peninnah up; one way or

Little Pearls of Wisdom...The Grace Chronicles

the other. Yet, even before Hannah got pregnant, she did not retaliate. Hannah did something totally opposite instead, which leads me into my second point. Hannah prayed. And there is nothing like prayer to silence the voice of the nay-sayers. Even after Hannah conceived and gave birth, she could have smudged Peninnah's face in her victory. But, nowhere in the scripture does it say that Hannah took revenge out on Peninnah. It was these silent lessons of Hannah that let me know that she was upright and walked in integrity. Do you know how hard it is to not 'take the bait?' Some days may be easier than others; especially if I did not pray that morning. So, to see Hannah, not 'take the bait' when she had every right to silence the mouth of Peninnah, was admirable. Admirable because regardless of Hannah's own circumstances, she stayed humble. Regardless of the mockery she was receiving, she stayed humble. Regardless of how inadequate she may have felt, she stayed humble. And, in her humility, in her trust in God, in her faith in God, God exalted her. God prepared a table for Hannah right in the presence of her enemy. That right there is a shouting moment! A shouting moment because I know that God is no respecter of persons, and what He does for one, He is able to do for me!

    Now, fast paced moving forward, Hannah's baby boy, Samuel, is now a man. Samuel is a prophet of God, and he has been appointed by God to anoint

Beep. Beep. Beep. This Is Only A Test...

Israel's first king, Saul. During his reign, Saul became rebellious and disobedient. Therefore, God instructed Samuel to anoint a replacement king for Saul. The full story is found in 1 Samuel chapter 16. It is important to note that God never intended for the Israelites to desire a king because God thought Himself to be their King. However, they wanted to be like everyone else they saw. In other words, they were trying to keep up with the Jones'. Therefore, my next little *pearl* of wisdom is: "Stop trying to be like someone else. Stop trying to act like someone else. Stop doing what you see other people doing. God did not create you to be a replica of anyone, or anything else. You are His authentic original. When He created you, He said that you are fearfully and wonderfully made. So, stop allowing other people to define who God says you already are — His special possession (1 Peter 2:9)."

Now, getting back to Saul. Saul was the *people's* choice for a king and not *God's* choice. However, God gave the people what they asked for. Like many of us, sometimes we only want something because we see that somebody else has it. Or, sometimes we think that we *know* best and that we *know* what the most obvious, and best choice, should be. And, rather than asking, and waiting on God's report, sometimes we fall prey to following the consensus of the crowd. You know that crowd? The crowd who expects never to have to wait. However, it is this kind urgency that can lead you into pursuing man-ordained options and not God-ordained paths. Well, such was the case in the placement of king Saul. The people qualified him because they were looking at his outer existence. They were looking at those things that could be seen. His strength. His defeats. His strategies. His popularity. His victories. But God looks at so much more. He looks at the heart of man. Think about it like this. Looking at something from only the outside is like judging a book only by its cover. Reading the beginning or the ending, and just skipping over the middle. But honey, you are missing the best part. There is so much to be gained in the middle. So much can happen in the middle. It is in the middle that your character gets developed. It is in the middle where your integrity gets refined. It is in the middle that your trust gets stronger. It is in the middle that your obedience becomes more diligent. It is in the middle that your faith gets strengthened. And it is also in the middle where you see God's hand of grace over your life. It is in this middle where God sees your true intentions, where your heart gets exposed. And it is in this exposure of your heart that God looks at. Ding. Ding. Ding. This is what sets you apart. The pure posture of a man's heart. Have you examined the true intentions of your heart lately? This is what aided in the selection of king Saul's replacement. Because God is ever-seeing and all-knowing, the posture of David's heart to please God, was undeniable. This is what set him apart from Saul. This was the reason the prophet Samuel was told to anoint David as the new king. David's heart posture towards God never wavered. Yes, David made mistakes. But, even in his mistakes, David still longed for God to create in him a pure heart. A heart that would see Him more clearly. A heart that would take away the guilt of his shame. A heart that would renew a right spirit within him. A heart that would align with the purpose that God has for his life.

To most, David was probably *not* the most obvious choice in choosing a king. In fact, in comparison to his brothers, he was 'Least likely to be chosen.' However, God saw otherwise. How many people have ever voted you 'least likely to succeed?' How many people have ever counted you out because *they* did not think that you were qualified? The good thing is that it does not matter what man thinks, or does not think, it is God who calls you out and qualifies you. So, in knowing that when God calls you, He has already equipped you for the assignment.

In walking out my purpose, I am intent on evolving into a better woman, because of the little *pearls* of wisdom from people like Hannah, Samuel, and David. Here is another great and valuable little *pearl* of wisdom, "What God chooses does not always look like what man expects. I have seen God use the LEAST likely to do the MOST unexpected. Trust God's timing.

He knows exactly where to prepare the table!" I am learning that when God calls you for His purpose, you cannot look at what you do not have. You cannot look at what you may not be. You cannot look at your insufficiencies, your inadequacies, or your insecurities. And you definitely cannot look at God's timing because ten times out of ten, His timing is not going to be convenient for you. When God calls you, the answer should always be, "Yes God. Amen (2 Corinthians 1:20)." Man did not qualify you or me. God did! And, when God called you, He qualified you. Man examines your qualities, your strengths, your weaknesses. But God looks at your heart. He looked at Hannah's heart and He looked at David's heart. He looks at your desire to please Him. Your intentionality in going after Him. The same grace that God showed Hannah and David is the same grace I want to show to my brothers/sisters. So, one of my daily prayers has been for God to use me as a grace demonstrator. And what this means is that I desire to demonstrate more grace than I demonstrate judgment. I desire to demonstrate more mercy than I demonstrate condemnation. I desire to demonstrate more expressions of forgiveness than to demonstrate punishment. Instead of just talking the talk, my desire has been to intentionally and deliberately walk the walk. I want the fruit of my walk, my talk, and the demonstration of how I treat others to be the manifested evidence of the authenticity of

Beep. Beep. Beep. This Is Only A Test...

my God. How's that for *not* trying to keep up with the Jones'?

My last little *pearls* of wisdom to you are, "Stay true to who you are. Stay true to Whom you belong. Stay true to what you have been called to do. And trust that God will make the pieces of the puzzle of your life fit together. Always remember that you are never too SMALL to do a BIG job in the Kingdom of God. His provisions will grace you for the task." I am going to leave you with this scripture from 2 Corinthians 3:5, which says, "It is not that we think we are qualified to do anything on our own. Our qualification comes from God." Period. I know you can't see me, but I just dropped the mic!

#TeamYou'veEarnedYourPearls

Fruit of the Spirit...

Dear God,
I pray Your grace
in being able to show
unconditional and unrestrained
love to everyone I meet. Give me
the **joy** of You and not of the world. Allow
Your **peace** to be like a fountain overflowing
inside of me. Let me not be stingy with the amount
of **patience** that I give. Let the words of my mouth speak
of Your unfailing **kindness**. Allow a continual flow of
Your **goodness** to manifest through me. Help me to
remain **faithful** to You, Your Word, Your people,
and to my assignment. Let my hands, my feet,
and my eyes demonstrate an unexplainable
compassion. And, as I travel life's journey,
help me to walk in **self-control** and
help my tongue to be ever so
careful to only **speak** life.
In Jesus' name I pray,
Amen...

Galatians 5:22-23

A Love Story *Unlike* Any Other...

For God so loved the world that He gave His one and only Son, that whoever believes in Him shall not perish but have eternal life...John 3:16

Love...

    I knew I was right where I was supposed to be when I started my very first day of ministry school. The plethora of information that I was being taught, shook my entire core. I had no idea the richness, the wealth, the intensity, of God's Word. I was just in awe. I developed a tenacity to just eat. Whether I was reading or listening to the Word, my appetite became insatiable. I couldn't get enough. I know that God's Word is living, but I didn't understand this revelation until around this time. Every time I submersed myself, I was always filled. I wanted, I had, to learn more because the more I learned about my Creator, the more I learned why I was created. I'm all in now. Not only was I becoming a Word 'junkie,' but I wanted to become a Word 'applier.' I didn't want to be just a *hear*-er of the Word, but I wanted to be a *do*-er of the Word (James 1:22). In my fascination of this 'new' world that I had recently discovered, notice I said, 'I discovered.' Sidebar: God's Word isn't something brand new. It has been around for years longer than I know. I just had to develop a hunger for it. But, getting back to my statement of this 'new' fascination that I had developed, I found myself wanting to learn more about Jesus. I know what He means to me, but I wanted to learn more about what He means to others as well. And, the different names/titles He is called. So, I started began studying. And, once I began, I realized that Jesus has many names/titles. For He is One to many and Many to one. If you will just humor me for a bit, I'd like to share with you some of these titles/names that I found, that were not among the more common ones that I have ever heard. One of these titles/names for Jesus is Consolation of Israel (Luke 2:25). There is Faithful and True Witness (Revelation 3:14), Heir of All Things (Hebrews 1:1-2), and Shiloh (Genesis 49:10). Some more titles/names are Man of Sorrow (Isaiah 53:3), Indescribable Gift (2 Corinthians 9:15), Arm of the Lord (Isaiah 53:1), Shepherd and Bishop of Souls (1 Peter 2:25), Dayspring (Luke 1:78), and Blessed and Only Potentate (1 Timothy 6:15). This list doesn't even scratch the surface of all the many names and the titles of Jesus. There was one name,

A Love Story Unlike Any Other...

however, I heard that just kept ringing in my spirit. This name is Redeemer. To be honest, I learned the 'cut and dry' version of what this name meant. Jesus redeemed us of our sins by taking our place on the cross. He paid the price to redeem us to eternal life. However, it wasn't until I read in the Book of Ruth that I learned another title/name for Jesus — Kinsman Redeemer. This intrigued me so I began studying and reading more intently. And the Holy Spirit showed me a perspective that I had never once contemplated. Please allow me to share with you what was shown to me.

A kinsman, in its simplest form, is *related* to you, usually by blood relation, by marriage, or by nationality or ethnic group. Now, a redeemer is one who buys back, or pays, the ransom for the release, or restoration, of someone or something. Thereby giving freedom from whatever form of captivity they were in. There are three criteria which must be taken into consideration for a person to be qualified as a kinsman redeemer: 1) A kinsman redeemer must be w*illing* to redeem. 2) A kinsman redeemer must have a *right* to redeem. And 3) A kinsman redeemer must have the *power*, *authority*, and *means* to redeem. Without all these standards being met, a person may not be eligible to be considered a redeemer. Before delving in, I used to think that the Book of Ruth was just another 'underdog-type' of love story. Ruth, being this poor and widowed 'underdog,' was rescued, or saved, by this rich man who gave her everything. What's interesting about that? Man sees woman. Man is intrigued by woman. Man falls for woman. Man takes woman as his wife. They have children. Life is good. End of story. Short and sweet. But au contraire. The Book of Ruth is not just a book Naomi, Ruth, and Boaz, but it is a shadow and type of Jesus Christ.

The Book of Ruth is an Old Testament example of what's called a type and shadow, of the New Testament. Types are used to denote a resemblance between something present and something future. And shadows are the same as types, in that they represent an Old Testament entity that foreshadows a New Testament truth. Here's a little example of shadows and types, and the parallelisms they share. Let's take, for example, the story of Joseph, the favored son of Jacob (Israel) can be found in Genesis. Many characteristics of Joseph's life, first mentioned in the Old Testament, were very similar to the life lived by Jesus Christ, which has been recorded in the New Testament. Let's delve a little deeper into these shadows and types between Joseph and Jesus: 1) Joseph was a shepherd (Genesis 37:2); as was Jesus (John 10:11), 2) Joseph 'redeemed' his nation (Genesis 4:37-44); as did Jesus (Isaiah 44:22), 3) Joseph was hated by his brothers (Genesis 37:3-4); as was Jesus (John 1:11), 4) Joseph was betrayed and sold for pieces of silver (Genesis 37:20-36); as was Jesus (Matthew 26:15), 5)

A Love Story Unlike Any Other...

Joseph was falsely accused and imprisoned (Genesis 39:6-21); as was Jesus (Luke 23:2-3), 6) Joseph was assumed to be dead and was not recognized when seen alive (Genesis 42:6-9); as was Jesus (Luke 24:36-42), and 7) Joseph was exalted after suffering greatly (Genesis 41:39-42); as was Jesus (Hebrews 2:9). The one key element to remember about shadows and types is that The Old Testament conceals that which the New Testament reveals. And the New Testament reveal that which the Old Testament conceal. My hope is that you have a little better understanding of shadows and types, because this will be most helpful in our continuation of the ultimate love story found in the Book of Ruth.

At first glance, you immediately notice the actual size of this book. It is a noticeably short, bite-sized book in the Bible, a whole whopping four chapters. However, don't be deceived by the size. For we all know that dynamite comes in small packages. If you've ever read the Song of Solomon, one might agree that the intimacy and romanticism, shared between the couple, contained in this book, is breath-taking. But it was something differently special about the Book of Ruth. This book enveloped you. It exemplified a love unlike any other. If you are a romantic, you would call this the 'ultimate love story.' However, this is not just a typical love story between two individuals. This is a sacrificial-type of love story. An unblemished type of love story. A 'grace covers all' type of love story between us and Our Sovereign Father.

Now, I hope you're better understanding the correlation between how the story of Boaz and Ruth is a shadow and type of redemption. The way Boaz became Ruth's kinsman redeemer is the same way that Jesus became our Kinsman Redeemer. Jesus checked all the boxes, as far as fitting the qualifications, in order to redeem us back unto God. Jesus is our Kinsman Redeemer, who bought and paid the cost, for our redemption. And it is from this exchange (i.e., He took our place so we wouldn't have to), we were delivered, liberated, and freed from having to face the penalty of sin. As a result of this personal business transaction, we (i.e., sinners) have been reconciled and redeemed. This is why Jesus came because this transaction had to be personal in order for Him to be relatable to us. Jesus came and so graciously took our place on the cross so we wouldn't have to. Jesus came and so graciously solidified the deal of salvation (i.e., redemption) so that we could be restored back into the family of God as sons. Jesus came to put us back in right relationship with God, Our Father. For Galatians 3:26 says, "For you are all sons of God through faith in Christ Jesus."

Although the players are few in the Book of Ruth, everyone plays a crucial part. We've explored an aspect of Ruth's importance. Now, let's take a look at

A Love Story Unlike Any Other...

Naomi. To a person looking at her situation from the outside in, it may look like Naomi did not, and should not, have anything to be grateful for. She had lost her husband and her two sons. And, in the process of her grief, she even lost herself. She changed her name from Naomi, which means companion, friend, or vision of beauty to Mara; a name which means sad or bitter (Ruth 1:20). My first little *pearl* of wisdom is to never answer to anything except your name. Never allow something you go through to change your name. You are not your condition. The challenges we go through are only temporary. Your situation cannot last always. For weeping only endures for a moment, but joy will come in the morning." If you give up now, you will forfeit your morning!

My second little *pearl* of wisdom is a little 'fill in the blank' quiz that the Holy Spirit gave me. It's really quite simple. The objective is to just fill in the blank of the sentence, "God will *never* _____." The foundational scripture I was given was Numbers 23:19, "God is not a man, so He does not lie." How 'bout we take this for a run? Psst...It's not to convince me, this is more so for you. Smile. God will *never* leave you or forsake you (Deuteronomy 31:8). God will *never* leave you alone (Joshua 1:9). God will *never* tempt you beyond what you are able to bear (1 Corinthians 10:13). God will *never* deal with us as our sins deserve (Psalm 103:10). God will *never* let the cries of His children go unheard

(Psalm 34:17). God will *never* let the prayers of the righteous fall to the wayside (Proverbs 15:29). God will *never* leave you weary, without being the wings to lift you up (Isaiah 40:31). God will *never* leave you hungry, without giving you Bread of Life (John 6:51). God will *never* leave you dry, without providing you with Living Water (John 7:37-39). God will *never* leave you empty, without quenching your thirst (John 4:14). God will *never* allow something to be taken away from you, without replacing it (Job 42:10). God will *never* manipulate His mercy (Psalm 100:5). God will *never* abandon His children from His grace (Romans 3:24). God will *never* allow His children to be defeated by the enemy (1 John 4:4). God will *never* leave you broken without being One who is able to restore (Psalm 147:3). God will *never* let you start something that He is not able to finish (Hebrews 12:2). Or, just to seal the deal, God will *never* take back His love (Psalm 118:1). I could keep on going, but I feel you got the jist. The bottom line goes back to two little, yet profound, words beginning the original scripture, "God is." Not God *never*, but God *IS*. God is everything in all things and there isn't anything that He is not. Period.

    Do you know why I use these narratives from the Bible? These testimonies of others? God left us a blueprint to try and help us get to know who He is, and how Omnipotent He is. If He is the same God yesterday that He is today, then I am pretty sure He will be the same

God tomorrow. These narratives are not for entertainment, but they were left so that we would know the integrity of God. They were left to be a road map of encouragement; knowing that if He did it for one, then He is able to do it for me. If God, showed Himself strong *then*, and I'm sharing my testimony with you, affirming His faithfulness *now*, what would make you question His Sovereignty? God is no respecter of persons, only of principle. That, in itself, should be encouragement that He is able to do what He did then for you *today*, if you're following the same principle. The experiences that I have been through in my life will only take you so far. I am not the standard. However, I can attest to the Standard being His written Word. God is a God of demonstration, and His Word provides us with such. All He asks is that you believe, and walk, in the footprints that He left behind.

There is always a bigger picture with God and I'm going to let you in on a little secret...chances are, you may not always know what God's plan is. But just know, He has one. Whew! I'm glad to get that off my chest. God *always* has a bigger plan than what we can see or fathom. A plan of which we are not always aware. A plan that He is working on behind the scenes. A plan that is leading to your restoration and His glorification. You *never* know what God has in store for you right around the corner. He can take you from gleaning in the field to owning the field, without delay.

Just ask Ruth! However, there is a requirement. And the requirement is faith. I am pretty sure there were countless times when Naomi wanted to quit and throw in the towel, but she did not. She held onto her faith. Somehow, I believe that deep down, even though things in her life had not worked out how she thought they would. Even though it looked like she had lost everything. Even though she did not always have what she thought she needed, she persevered. And, because of her faith to persevere, God opened a window from heaven and poured out a blessing that she did not have room enough to receive. I am not even talking so much about the *tangible* things that were restored back to her. Like for instance: her property, her land, and her home. But I am talking about those things that she was able to display that money could not buy. I am talking about her peace of mind, her value in herself, and her worth in how she looked at herself. Naomi could look at her reflection and not judge herself by what she had been through. She could look at her reflection and not smell the stench of her condition, or the circumstances of where she thought that life had abandoned her. Her heart was not burdened, broken, or as heavy as it used to be. Naomi could actually smile again. Smile again because she was given another chance at motherhood, in helping to raise Ruth and Boaz's son. Through her trials and tribulation, her faith and trust in God was strengthened. And the joy that the world tried to take away from her, God restored it back unto her, immeasurably. She got her laughter back, her dance back, her name back, her life back. If you have never lost some of these *intangibles* before, then they may not be as priceless you as the next woman. However, to those of you that have, we can stand in agreement, and boldly declare, that God will never allow something to be stripped from you that He is not able to replace and restore one-hundred-fold over.

If I could leave you with this little *pearl* of wisdom, it is only two words, but it is two words that reminds me that God's *always* has His eye on me. This is a title/name that God is called — El Roi, which means God sees you. One of the most infamous tricks that the enemy uses on us is to tell us that God has forgotten about us. Well, that is a flat out lie! Come on now. If God took the time to number, not count, but number the hairs on your head, you do not think He always knows your exact location (Numbers 12:7)? We put these microchips in our pets so if they get lost, we can easily locate them. If we, as pet owners, put that much investment in something that we did not create, why wouldn't you think that God would not put *at least* that much investment in the *things* (i.e., 'Us') that He created in His own image (Genesis 1:27)? Silly rabbit, those tricks are for kids!

Sometimes, it may look like everyone else had a head-start on Naomi and Ruth. You may even have felt like this before, I know I have. But, from my own testimony, I have seen God thrust me past everyone, ahead of the game. The same way He did Ruth. She went from employee to employer, from worker to owner, from the bottom to the top, from renter to owner. My last little pearl of wisdom is: "Stay true to who you are and what God has called you to. 'You' are your own starting point, and not anyone else. You cannot look at where the next person is or is not. You run your race. You stay your course. You respect your own authenticity. You embrace your own originality. No one can be a better version of you, than 'You.'" I will leave you with this scripture from Hebrews 12:1-3, which says, "We must run the race that lies ahead of us and never give up. We must focus on Jesus, the source and goal of our faith." Faith is accessible to all. And, it is by faith, that we are adopted into *son*-ship (gender *in*-specific) of God Most High. Is your adoption still open? Or have you signed on the dotted line? God redeemed us, through Christ, to be His forever children. Have you chosen Him to be your Forever Father?

#TeamWalkingWithMyPearlsOfGrace

5

Ready. Set. Go. Wardrobe Change...

You brought me up from the grave, O Lord. You kept me from falling into the pit of death. You have turned my mourning into joyful dancing. You have taken away my clothes of mourning and clothed me with joy, that I might sing praises to You and not be silent. O Lord my God, I will give You thanks forever!...Psalm 30:3, 11-12

Joy

Hi. My name is Tena and here is my transparency moment: As a little girl, and even into my adulthood, I sometimes struggled with embracing my own self-image. I think somewhere along the way, I got so focused on who others thought I should be, and I ended up trying to please everyone else and live up to their expectations of 'Me.' And, please let's not even mention how tv or social media defines what a growing, impressionable little girl should look like. So many *(wrong)* choices to choose from. What was a girl to do? You may have an easy answer, but as you can tell, I did not. I was like a chameleon, and I just tried to fit in where I could get in. And that was even difficult at times. I can remember looking at the qualities that other women had, wondering why I did not really look like any of them. Why was that? What was wrong with me? Why was it so hard for me to fit the 'norm?' Why wasn't I comfortable just being 'Me?' And why did I feel the need to imitate or be like anyone else, other than myself? Before we delve into this, it is important that I share this scripture with you. It was a scripture that will not help you, but I know it will bless you. It is found in Ephesians 1:6, "To the praise of the glory of His grace, wherein He hath made us accepted in the Beloved." For anyone who has ever struggled with their identity, their self-image, trying to fit in, or just plain old puberty, this scripture tells you who you are in Him. This scripture gives you your identity, in Christ, when you have had troubles finding your own. This scripture tells you that you do not have to be accepted by anyone because the Beloved (i.e., Jesus) has sealed and stamped you 'accepted.' And, because you have already been branded 'accepted,' you already have your identity. So, you do not have to be bound to anyone's perception, or ideas, of how you should be. God made the necessary *pro*-vision, for you and for me, to have access. Ephesians 3:12

states, "In whom we have boldness and access with confidence by the faith of Him." Your access does not come from what others say it should be. Your access does not come from anything that you might have done. But your access comes from having faith in Him. In Him, we have the access to the identity that He says is ours. In Him, we have access to be who He has called us to be. In Him, we have access to be delivered from the expectations of others! Therefore, my first little *pearl* of wisdom is to know that you have access! The Bible says that we have boldness and access, with that dynamic duo on our side, I see why now the enemy did everything in his power to keep me ignorant from knowing that I have access. He should have kept me in the dark. Because now since I know better, not only am I going to do better, but I am going to tell anyone who will listen — God is the One who gave us our identity in Him. It is by faith whether or not you receive it. If you choose to believe, I only have two words for you — *access granted!*

I did not know just how flawed my own self-image was; that is until I realized how much of it had been shattered. I discuss this in great detail in a few of my earlier books. But, just to give an overview, until you get the other books, that is, I will share a little bit with you. Smile. I would first like to say that I am saddened that my story is not that uncommon. Some of you may even be able to relate. Allow me to just say is that my story is not my excuse. It is just my story — truthful and transparent. I do not believe that there was a right or wrong for me to respond. I am just sharing how I did. And, as a result, you will see some of the consequences and effects that resulted from my responses. I did not know it at the time, but my innocence had been perverted; thereby leading to me having some skewed responses about affection, affirmation, intimacy, and sexual intercourse; to name a few.

My 'real' dysfunction began in my pre-pubescent years, and like many other young black girls, my father was also absentee; which unknowingly contributed to the wall I had built around my heart. I know now that I needed my Daddy to show me what a man looks like and how a man is supposed to treat me. But, even bigger than that, I needed my Daddy to show me how I was supposed to treat a man. It is a two-way street ladies, so do not think this isn't important as well. How you feel about yourself, not how you look or the woman you try to portray, but how you *really* feel about that little girl staring back at you in the mirror, comes out in your actions. It dictates how you treat others. So, if you have a nasty attitude, it will show in how you treat people. Just chew on that for a minute. As little girls, we need our Daddy's for more than one reason. They are an integral part of our growth, self-esteem, and self-image. I cannot make a generalized

Ready. Set. Go. Wardrobe Change...

statement and say that all women need this, but in my case, I did. I needed my father to validate my identity. I needed my father to put his 'stamp' on me. His 'stamp' of approval. His 'stamp' telling me that he would always love me no matter what. His 'stamp' telling me that he would always encourage me. His 'stamp' supporting me, that no matter happened in life, through my good decisions as well as my bad decisions, he would still say, and see me, as being his valuable little girl.

I am not 'Daddy bashing' because I loved that handsome 'Sun duster' (i.e., my Daddy), and I was ret-to-fight anytime anyone would put their mouth on him. I am just trying to make you understand that being 'Daddy's little girl' was something that I longed for and needed; not even realizing it. We did not have this relationship as I was growing up, however, God in Him mercy, allowed us to mend all the broken ties that had separated us. And, from that day forward, at 28 years old, until the day he closed his eyes and breath left his body, I was a 'Daddy's girl.'

I am not going to put the entire blame on my 'Daddy issues,' but it was from this that my view of myself was not what it should have been. Oftentimes, I would struggle with feelings of unworthiness, feeling unvalued, abandoned, rejected, neglected, and unloved. I felt like the scum on the bottom of your shoe because as a child, I just did not understand why the man who had helped to create me, wanted very little to do with me. So, having a positive self-esteem? No ma'am, not at all. I did not have that at all. And when I thought I could not feel any worse. Boy was I wrong. I may not have been the apple of my Daddy's eye, but I became the apple of someone else's eye. Hence, my introduction to molestation. Oh, how the plot thickens. As if I was not already becoming more broken and more damaged, now I am trying to sift through feelings of being ashamed, embarrassed, and feeling dirty. If invisibility were a mathematical value, I would have been like invisible squared! I was a hot mess, and I did not even know it. That is, until these repressed emotions and feelings, that I had securely locked up in the treasure chest of my heart, began to show up in my relationships, especially my marriage.

    If any of you were thinking, "Where was her mother when all of this was going on?" Well, I am glad you asked. I was raised by a beautiful, strong, intelligent Black woman who sacrificed everything for her kids. Many times, she went last so that we could go first. She managed to send all three of her children to college and we each hold at least a bachelor's degree. So, my mother did pretty darn good. She was a mother and a father to us all. And she absolutely did the best that she knew how to do with the cards that she was dealt. However, this woman had *absolutely* no idea what was going with me. I never said a word.

Ready. Set. Go. Wardrobe Change...

I have always been kind of shy and non-talkative. It was not until I let it 'slip' out in a conversation all the things that I had been struggling with. So, I know if she had known the struggles that I was going through, she would have moved heaven and earth for me. But what she did not know, she could not address because I never shared. Like I said, I have always been a kind of shy and reserved person, but I was well into my adult years when I was beginning to understand more of the dynamics as to why my personality was as such. I was not always reserved because I can remember being a bubbly child who loved playing practical jokes on people. I am a 'reaction' person and I love to see those expressions on a person's face. But I slowly began losing my smile and my laughter. And I became kind of introverted. Should this have been a 'red flag,' maybe. However, growing up in the 1970's, was a different time than what we have now. Today, thankfully, we have more access (there is that word again) to a lot more resources, education, and training than what we had back then. Needless to say, there came a time in my life where it became pivotal whether I was going to choose to either live or die (not physically). So, I chose 'living' for $200 Alex. And I realized that a lot of the shyness that I had developed came from being insecure. Insecure about being 'Me;' whatever that meant. Like with other women who have been through early childhood trauma, you develop a 'coping' and/or defense mechanism. And my coping mechanism was to compartmentalize and just 'sweep things under the rug.' However, my defense mechanism was building a wall around my heart to protect it from any further hurt. In my childhood mind, if I hid it, then it did not happen. And, I would never have to address, confront, or deal with it. If I hid it, then maybe I could just put some flowers on that pile of 'mess' and act like it was a part of the decorative furniture. However, *none* of my brilliant ideas worked. The only thing that worked was confronting it. So, this has been my season of exposure, transparency, and truth, and learning that whatever did not break me, only strengthened, and grew me.

So far, I have only talked about what was happening within me, now it is time to shift to what was happening outside of me. Yes, I had physical insecurities as well. If you did not realize it by now, this is what I like to call my 'couch time' (therapy time) that I am allowing you to be a part of. Hope you do not mind listening? Smile. Getting back to my physical insecurities. I am what I like to call 'non-vertically blessed.' I did not have a problem with it but seemed like everyone else did. Therefore, it became *my* physical insecurity. Allow me to interject my second little *pearl* of wisdom, "Do not let someone else's insecurity become your own. When they try to deliver that mail to your address, to your house, you write on that, 'Return to sender,' and go about your day. Their issues are their issues. Do not let them try to pass along what they struggle with to you. Trust me, we have enough to deal with on our own." Back to my physical insecurities. Along with being a little chubby with a big forehead, small feet, and crooked teeth, I had also lost my hair in the fourth grade. To God be the glory for Jeri curls because ya' girl had to rock one sooner than anyone else! People thought that I was trying to be a 'fashionista' or something, but my mama was just trying to stop her baby girl from having to walk around shiny-scalped! These were some tough times. But, to God be the glory! Because He is using everything that I went through for my testimony and His glory!

If I could go back in time and give the little girl version of me a message, I would tell her, "The enemy is trying to kill your spirit baby girl. He does not want you to know that God has given you access in Him baby girl. God has not forgotten about you. It is just the opposite. He loves you so much that He put something on the inside of you, beforehand, for you to use know. Keep believing in Him and know that you have been and are always on God's mind." However, somewhere along the lines, I missed the memo. But I know now! And I am full speed ahead. I can rest my hat knowing that God does not make mistakes. And that goes for His timing as well. Everything happens for a reason, and everything happens in its season. Who knows where I would be? If I allowed myself to get stuck on the 'what if's,' that is right where I will be, stuck. I cannot change anything that I have done, but I am willing to be affective in the things that I am going to do. I am, "Forgetting what is behind and reaching forward to what is ahead, I pursue as my goal the prize promised by God's heavenly call in Christ Jesus (Philippians 3:13-14)."

If I do not know anything else, I know that change happens first *within* you. You may not be able to change your situation or even the players involved, but you can change how you respond to it and them. Which leads me to my next little *pearl* of wisdom that I would like to offer, "Never let your growth be dependent on the temperature of others. Only you can control what you do. Do not give anyone that right, or privilege, of dictating your emotions, regardless of the situation. Confront it. Accept it. Process it. Work through it. And do not forget to exhale in between. If you do your part in the natural, God will meet you with His super. And watch His strength stand up in your weakness."

Recently, something out of the ordinary happened to me. I received a message from a male acquaintance who I do not normally talk to, other than in social settings. So, receiving a message from this person was quite different. This person, however, sent me an article to read. Now initially, I did not pay much attention to the article because I was at work. But when this person messaged me to get my thoughts on it, I realized they wanted an 'on the spot' response. Normally, I may would have still responded later, but for some reason, I felt an urgency to respond to receive a message from this person was out of the ordinary. So, I knew that it was something bigger than what it looked like on the surface. Considering that this acquaintance reached out to me at all, said a lot. Also, I felt the urgency to respond because this guy was really concerned when he read this article. And he needed a female's perspective on it. I was humbled. So, I wanted to earnestly address his concern. If I may add, I was feeling some kind of way with my response. Mainly because he knows how I flow. He knows I believe in God, and I try to live my life representing that. We have never even had a conversation about his beliefs, but he was very aware of mine. But, if I am being honest, him asking my thoughts kind of caught me off-guard that day. But I was obedient because when you walk with God, you cannot be skeptical about how He chooses to speak. I knew this conversation was God-ordained because you will not believe what the article was about? It was about how society tries to impose an unrealistic stereotype on the self-image of women of color. Cha-ching! I was ready. This was an opportunity to share not just my testimony, but it gave me an opportunity to put God on a pedestal! Now, this guy had no idea the struggles that I have had in this area. This guy had no idea the struggles that other women of color may have had in this area as well. But here I was, being given the platform to speak on something that not only have I held dear but can share my true thoughts from personal experience; to hopefully uplift the next woman. Here again, God's timing may not be my timing, but His timing is *always* right on time!

Before I begin my share of what I told him, I would first like to say that as much as I hear people say, 'I don't see color,' I do. I was born a woman of color and I will die a woman of color. That is not going to change. However, what I can change is how I view people. I treat people how I want to be treated, regardless of color. If someone is rude, it does not matter their color. They are just rude! But getting back to this article. As I was reading, at first, I did not know what I was going to say. Sidebar: I recently had the opportunity to do a YouTube interview with 'This Week in America' with Ric Bratton, for my second book, "Growing Up In Marriage...Perfectly Flawed." If I tell you that I was nervous, like days before, would be an understatement. I remember praying and asking the Holy Spirit to be my mouthpiece because this was not my moment. It was His. I figured since the Holy Spirit had given me the words to write, I needed Him to also give me the words to say. The clock was winding down and it was getting closer and closer to my interview. I

Ready. Set. Go. Wardrobe Change...

was trying not to be nervous, but I was a little. Psst... Do not forget about God's timing. It was like the Holy Spirit waited until I opened my mouth and used my voice to speak, that He began talking. I cannot explain the peace I had as I was doing this interview. Me? Speaking in front of people? Not 'Me?' The shy, reserved, and insecure little girl? No one could have told me that I would have been able to do that. But the evidence is there. The proof is in the pudding because the interview is out there on YouTube. I said all that to say this, "Just like with my interview, the Holy Spirit didn't begin speaking until I first opened my mouth and began speaking." Another little *pearl* of wisdom is, "Do your part in the natural and God will do His part in the super." Once I began responding to my friend's request, the words just began flowing. I did not realize how impactful this whole idea of self-image had affected me. I said a whole lot of things, but the one thing that I remember saying is that life is sometimes unfair in how it may treat you. And, as children, we do not always know the best way to handle things. But it is good to know that even those scars and wounds, won't stop your destiny. It becomes a part of it. Part of your strength. Part of your growth. This too, will become a part of your testimony. The things that we go through are not solely about us. It is about sharing your experiences with the next person. Did you know that has sent us lifelines — each other.

Little Pearls of Wisdom...The Grace Chronicles

We are here to encourage one another. We are here to support one another. We are here to beautify one another. We are here to love one another. And give each other the grace to walk in our truth.

Also, I expressed my concern on how in today's society, so many people focus on outer beauty. But beauty is only skin deep. There is nothing wrong with having a certain level of confidence about yourself. I get that and I encourage that. It just becomes a stumbling block when that is *all* you focus on. Self-worth (i.e., self-image/self-esteem) begins with loving the person that you are, flaws, scars, wounds, and all. Not the person that you are portraying, or displaying, in front of people. You know that 'displayed' person — the well-manicured/pedicured, face beat, hair slayed, fashionista kind of person, with no inner-substance whatsoever. What makes a woman beautiful is not what she is wearing, or even who she is wearing, but it is all about her attitude in knowing that she is of royal descent (1 Peter 2:9)!

When I talked earlier about my struggles in my youth, leading into my adulthood, the one thing you did not hear me mention was my countenance. Well, that is because I had not really embraced it. I did not know what it meant to love yourself. I did not know what it meant to value who you are, with or without validation or approval from my father. I did not know what it meant to appreciate the idea of being 'You;'

Ready. Set. Go. Wardrobe Change...

scars, flaws, and all. And I did not know what it meant to have joy in being the best version of myself. I had to learn that when God created me, He broke the mold baby! God was so outdone with His creation of 'Me' that He said, "I cannot do any better than this. Tena is my *authentic* original. This one right here. See, she is my perfect masterpiece (Ephesians 3:20)." I am not bragging; I am just being truthful. God loves me just like He loves you. Once you get that revelation deep down in your spirit, the enemy (using people, of course), will not be able to just treat you any old kind of way anymore. You are a King's kid. You are the apple of God's eye (Psalm 17:8). You are His beloved. Want to know how I know? Because He not only tells me, but God shows me every single day. Every day I open my eyes to see all that He is created for my pleasure, all that He is showing me. Every day when I am awakened by the birds singing outside of my bedroom window, serenading me saying, "Wake up Tena. It is time to get our day started. Wake up Tena. We have got work to do," He's telling me. Every day when I inhale and exhale. Like clockwork, my lungs involuntarily inflate and deflate, He is showing me that He's given me another day; another chance to walk in my assignment. Every day when I look up at the sun, shielded by the clouds in the sky, He is showing me that He's got me covered. He's given me the sun to guide me by day and the clouds to protect me from overheating from its rays and brightness. God's got me! And He has you too! And, just knowing that God has got me, gives me an unspeakable joy! A joy that I did not always feel. A joy that was smothered for a long time. A joy that can never be taken away from me. A joy that I delight myself in every day.

As I began my journey of walking with God, there was this one scripture that I would always gravitate back to; and I did not understand why until now. I like the entire chapter of Psalm 37, but I am only going to focus on verses 1-7, which reads, "Do not be agitated by evildoers (those who do wrong by you); do not envy those who do wrong. For they wither quickly like grass and wilt like tender green plants. Trust in the Lord and do what is good; dwell in the land and live securely. Take delight in the Lord, and He will give you your heart's desires. Commit your way to the Lord; trust in Him, and He will act, making your righteousness shine like the dawn, your justice like the noonday." In so many words, this verse is saying: 1) Trust in the Lord, 2) Delight yourself in the Lord, and 3) Commit your way to the Lord. And, let Him handle the rest. He has a way of succeeding any of your thoughts, imaginations, ideas, suggestions, goals, and plans, all for His glory!

Another little *pearl* of wisdom is similarly related to the previous pearl. What this verse ministers to me is to *never* let anyone steal your joy! It does

Ready. Set. Go. Wardrobe Change...

not matter what happens to you. It does not matter what people do to you. It does not matter the things that you may go through, no one, and I mean no one, should be entitled to steal your joy. Do not give them that right! Life will be full of ups and down, twists and turns, jerks and abrupt stops, heartbreak, and pain, but God. There is nothing that God allows that will be used to overtake you. In fact, He promised in His Word that even though the weapons form, none of them which comes up against you shall prosper. And any tongue that rises up against you will be condemned. This is our heritage as God's children (Isaiah 54:17). So, if God can guarantee that you will *not* be harmed, even though the weapon may form, then you must know that He has obviously already allotted for our every set-back, every misstep, every delay, and every wrong turn. It took me a while to grasp that God has His own timing. And what He wants to happen, will happen, when He is ready for it to happen. This gives me an assurance in knowing that God uses my setbacks as my set-ups. And, in the process of hoping and expecting, He will fill me with joy and peace in Him. I just have to put my trust in Him, so that I may overflow with hope (Romans 15:13).

My last little *pearl* of wisdom is to let you know that what you think, shapes your world. What you speak, shapes your world. What you believe, shapes your world. So, it *does* matter how you see yourself, how you speak to yourself, and what you believe about yourself. Proverbs 18:21 says "Death and life are in the power of the tongue: and they that love it shall eat the fruit thereof."

    Now, going forward, I am continually working on how to be...To be the woman that has accepted God's purpose for her life. To be the woman of integrity that God says that I am. To be the woman who understands how important it is to show grace because I am shown grace. To be the woman who not just talks faith, but actually walks by faith. To be the woman who shares her story to lift others up. To be the woman to share the little *pearls* of wisdom that I have gathered along the way. To be the woman to share the message of how God's undeserved gift of grace covers our life.

#TeamJoyToTheLord

6

The Silent Lessons Of A Praying Grandmother...

But the wisdom from above is first of all pure. It is also peace loving, gentle at all times, and willing to yield to others. It is full of mercy and the fruit of good deeds. It shows no favoritism and is always sincere...James 3:17

Peace...

If someone were to ask me to describe what I believed constituted being a woman, hands down, I would have one word — Doris. Doris is my maternal grandmother and as a little girl growing up, in my eyes, she was so beautiful — inside and out. Although I had self-esteem issues growing up, I did not realize that she was what kept me grounded. I was so fascinated with her essence of being a woman. To me, she was like the epitome of what I believed a woman looked like. She was a strong woman of God who not just taught compassion but lived it every single day. It did not matter the time, day, or night, all you had to do was call her and she would be there. This woman would give you her last, even if it were the shoes off her feet. My grandmother had a certain essence and grace about her as she entered any room. She had this high soprano voice when she sang that sounded like baby birds chirping. It was so melodic. And, she was always smiling, even when she called herself 'fussing.' I cannot recall too many times when I ever heard her raise her voice, yell, or shout. Her professional trade was that of a nurse, but that nurturing and caring type of demeanor escorted her wherever she went. For lack of a better description, it was almost like she was always in character. And I rarely, if ever, saw her forget her lines or not come in on cue. I loved the daintiness from how she walked to how she held her teacup. From the way she took care of her skin, her hair and nails, her clothing, and her body. One of her favorite perfumes was called Emeraude and it used to smell so good on her. Her skin was flawless, and it was always so smooth and soft. I watched her, not realizing how much I wanted to mimic her. So, I would do a lot of the things that I saw her do; from not putting a razor to her skin, to using sweet, fragrant, aroma-smelling bubble bath. One of her favorites was called Calgon. I remember watching the commercial and it would advertise this woman having, what looked to be, an incredibly stressful day. It was like she was hustling and bustling all day at work and her traffic commute was

The Silent Lessons Of A Praying Grandmother...

horrendous both driving to and from work. By the time she made it home, the kids were pulling at her the minute she walked in the front door; excited and anticipated to tell her about their day at school. All the while, waiting to greet her husband and the first words out of his mouth were, "What's for dinner honey?" Needless to say, this woman was absolutely crazy, but amazing. How she managed to do all this in just a matter of a two-to-three-minute commercial reel was just baffling to me. But do you want to know something funny? The commercial was not about this woman and the many hats that she wore. This commercial was not about how this woman was broadcasting her skills of how she managed time. This commercial was not about how flexible, tough, and resilient women are. This commercial was not even promoting how, I am sure, this woman may have wanted to lock everybody downstairs in the basement, just to get a moment of peace. But this commercial was promoting a bubble bath — Calgon. Really? A bubble bath? After this long and stressful day, after fulfilling all the obligations that were expected of her, after tending to everyone else's needs and then her own, all she had to do was let 'Calgon, take her away' and everything would be all right. I would watch my grandmother, who do not forget, never raised her voice and was always so mild-mannered, coupled with this bubble bath, I was for sure that I had found my remedy for life! I used to wonder why my grandmother used this product. She did not need to escape from us, life, or anything. We have always been such good children. LOL.

It is amazing how the mind equates things. I remember when I thought that I was grown, with 'tween' problems, I would take these Calgon baths. After discussing some of my childhood struggles from the previous chapter, I was trying to 'wash off' other things. However, the commercial advertised that this amazing product would give you the peace, tranquility, cleanliness, and rest that your body needed. I was all for it! It just did not give me the sense of cleanliness and peace that I was looking for. I was looking to get out of the tub free and lightweight and the issue that I was dealing with before the bath, is 'washed off' and going down the drain. I wanted to see all my troubles float and swirl far away. But that was not how it happened. As opposed to just watching her, I should have asked my grandmother, "What is the secret to your peace?" Because I later found out that it surely was not this powdered mix bubble bath.

If you live in this world, the one thing that none of us are exempt from is trouble. Trouble is no respecter of persons. Trouble is like that Miley Cyrus song; it comes in as an equal opportunity 'Wrecking Ball.' Trouble comes to the righteous, as well as the unrighteous. Trouble comes to the Believer, as well as the non-believer. Trouble comes to the just, as well as the unjust. I am not naive enough to believe that trouble will just skip over my house. It won't and it hasn't. But can I share with you what I now know was my grandmother's secret to her peace? Just like the one word which epitomizes what constituted being a woman, there is one word that epitomizes peace for me — Jesus. This was my grandmother's secret weapon! My grandmother was not a woman of *useless* words. And, when she did speak, it was impactful. Even though I would just watch her, some of her greatest messages to me were in the words that were not spoken. I did not realize it then and did not appreciate it as much as I should've, but I had a front-row seat of being able to watch the manifestation of the fruit of the Spirit manifest through my grandmother. She was the epitome of how I envisioned a woman should be; wounded, scarred, or flawed. My grandmother was not a wealthy woman, but she was spiritually rich. Rich in the blessings of the Lord. Proverbs 10:22 says, "The blessing of the Lord brings riches, and He adds no sorrow to it." Rich, in the sense that, she was overflowing in abundance, from the fruit of the Spirit that was within her. She was kind, compassionate, gentle, patient, and she was faithful to her calling (i.e., Ministry of helps/service; 1 Corinthians 12:28). She was never shaken or rattled (i.e., always displayed self-control). She always had a smile on her face and joy in her heart. And peace was like an aura around her. The lesson that my grandmother was teaching, and sowing into me, I did not appreciate it then. But the little *pearl* of wisdom that she was leaving me was learning how to live by the Spirit. And the only way that you can live by the Holy Spirit is if you allow Him to dwell in you and let Him manifest His fruit through you. That way, when trouble comes, He will direct you right on through it. Not that trouble won't come, but it is how you handle it when it does. And, if you did not know already, Psst...we have a secret weapon. We have an Advocate. We have a Paraclete on our side to help us *God*-vigate through life's troubles (John 14:26).

In this season of my life, I have been trying to utilize all the little *pearls* of wisdom that I am gathering along the way. And one of my little *pearls* is learning to stay sensitive to the Holy Spirit. There is a song that I have heard dozens of times. However, this one morning when I arose, I heard this song like I had never heard it before. The song is called I'm Available to You and I believe the original artist is Milton Brunson and The Thompson Community Singers. The lyrics are as follows:

The Silent Lessons Of A Praying Grandmother...

You gave me my hands to reach out to man
To show him Your love and Your perfect plan
You gave me my ears; I can hear Your voice so clear
I can hear the cries of sinners
But can I wipe away their tears?
You gave me my voice to speak Your Word
To sing all Your praises to those who never heard
But with my eyes I see a need for more availability
I've seen hearts that have been broken
So many people to be free
Lord, I'm available to You
My will I give to You
I'll do what You say do
Use me Lord to show someone the way
And enable me to say
My storage is empty, and I am available to You
Now I'm giving back to You
All the tools You gave to me
My hands, my ears, my voice, my eyes
So, You can use them as You please
I have emptied out my cup so that You can fill it up
Now I am free, I just want to be more available to You
Lord, I'm available to You
My will I give to You
I'll do what You say do
Use me Lord to show someone the way
And enable me to say
My storage is empty, and I am available to You

Little Pearls of Wisdom...The Grace Chronicles

As I began listening to the words in this song, an unspeakable peace come over me. That may not mean much to you, but at the time when I received this message in my spirit, there were so many distractions circling all around me. Distractions at work, distractions in my personal life, distractions with this person, distractions with that person, just distractions. And they were keeping me from being and staying focused. If I were a little girl all over again, I would think that I needed to take a Calgon bath. LOL. So, as the words of this song began ministering to me, I knew that God was sending me a message. A John 14:27 kind of message, "Peace I leave with you; My peace I give you. I do not give to you as the world gives. Do not let your hearts be troubled (i.e., distracted) and do not be afraid." After praying and meditating, I found myself yielding. Yielding all my distractions to God. Yielding all my gifts and talents to God. And, here is a big one — Yielding to God all of my plans and all expectations of anything that I had in mind. Yielding to His will, His way, and His plans and His purpose for my life. It is in this yielding, in this submission, where His peace is. It is in this place of trust, where I was able to find rest. It is in this place of comfort that I want to be available to Him. And, it is also in this yielding, that He will give you a kind of success that you did not even think was imaginable. The only success that matters — *God*-success.

The Silent Lessons Of A Praying Grandmother...

My last little *pearl* of wisdom that I would like to share is that there is a difference between being wealthy and being rich, and I am not talking monetary. Being rich is what I saw in my grandmother. No, she may not have always been able to go to the designer shopping stores or have the most expensive jewelry, but whatever she had, she made it look rich. And then my 'lightbulb moment' — Grandmama looking rich had nothing to do with the name brands she wore on the outside but looking rich had *everything* to do with the Name Brand (i.e., God's Line — the fruit of the Spirit) she clothed herself with on the inside. Grandmama had *God*-success. Now, the Bible talks about having *good* success in Joshua 1:3. That is not debatable. God's Word is sound. God's Word is rich. God's Word is unchanging. Nothing can be added to it. Nothing can be taken away from it. However, regarding the illustration that I was given, the Holy Spirit showed me a different perspective, or insight, on *God*-success and *good*-success. Maybe I was shown this because I did not know that there was such a thing. I thought success was success. And, I had measured the standard of what 'success' looked like based on the world's standards. But, if you will just stay open-minded, I will share with you what was shared with me. The world views success as going to college, getting your degree, landing a six-figured job, living in a prominent neighborhood,

Little Pearls of Wisdom...The Grace Chronicles

driving a brand-new car, being able to take trips and vacations whenever, and wherever, you wanted to go, wearing name-brand clothes, having expensive shoes and handbags, or wearing 10-karats on your finger. Do not get me wrong, if having 'things' equates success to you, then ride on and float that boat. I just have one question. After you get all that 'stuff,' vacation all over the world, go on shopping sprees in Milan and Paris, buy a garage full of exotic cars, have your own private jet, buy your own exclusive island, then what? Did the 'stuff' make you happy? Did the 'stuff' allow you to have nights of peaceful rest? Did the 'stuff' grow your patience? Did the 'stuff' give you more compassion and kindness towards people? I am not trying to be facetious for all these are rhetorical questions, just something to think about. For the *only* thing that can give you success, along with the fruit of the Holy Spirit, is God. He is the element that you should be rooting your success in, not 'stuff.' I get it, having 'stuff' quantifies your status on certain levels. It sets you apart. It tells the world that 'You have arrived. You have made it. You are 'bossing' it.' Arrived where? Made it where? Where did you get that standard? Who are you trying to keep up with? I am curious, tell me. What was the dollar amount, or the status quo, you reached when you dropped the mic and was like, "I am here. I can stop now. I have won." Was it when your bank account hit seven-figures?

The Silent Lessons Of A Praying Grandmother...

Was it when you bought that yacht? Was it when you paid cash for your house? Or was it when you called the dealership and asked them to open just for you? Tell me, what was that last deal you made that sent you over into 'Elite status?' I know that may have been a little over the top. To someone like myself, having the privilege of being able to do any of these things makes one look *highly* successful. I may not get a whole of 'Amens' for this next statement, but I am saying it anyway. Sometimes when a person reaches a certain status level, they somehow believe that they are untouchable or invincible. They credit themselves for all their hard work. And they should because they were the one putting in the long hours. The problem I have is that they stand on their platform all by themself. They take full credit for their success. I agree that they should get credit, however, I also believe that God, somewhere in the picture, should be getting the glory. Allow me to back-up my statement. Let me just put up my checklist: God created Person XX. God gave Person XX the skills, talent, creativity, and ambition to succeed. God opened doors for Person XX. God has given Person XX favor with men (gender neutral). God is sustaining Person XX with good health and strength to be able to do the job. God is keeping the mental faculties of Person XX intact. God is continually trying to get the attention of Person XX throughout the day, but Person XX still believes it is him who is thriving.

Yet, God is still providing Person XX with their daily bread. God has a band of angels shielding Person XX from attacks of the enemy. God has/is/will continue to do His thing for Person XX, even though Person XX does not even acknowledge Him or say, 'Thank You.' God loves Person XX and is waiting on them to have faith enough to believe that it is only because of His grace that they have made it thus far.

The world can paint a pretty picture of what their perspective of what 'success' looks like. But who's report are you willing to believe — God's or the worlds? Later rather than sooner, I was beginning to understand that not all *good*-success is *God*-success, and that there *is* a difference. If God is *not* the foundation of everything that you do, trust me, it will not last. *Newsflash*: Did you know that being successful really has nothing to do with you? You are just the vessel that God has chosen to display His glory in the earth. And, when the glory of God is evident in your life, this creates a different kind of platform than before, a platform where you step down and God steps up. A platform where you reach down and pull another woman up. A platform whereas God can be lifted up and all men shall be drawn (John 12:32). Not to your accomplishments or 'successes,' but to the God who has given you the ability to attain your accomplishments. A platform for you to testify of the God who has given you 1 Timothy 6:17, "Teach those who are rich in this world not to be proud and not to trust in their money, which is so unreliable. Their trust should be in God, who richly gives us all we need for our enjoyment."

So, knowing that God could use anyone to do whatever He wants to do, whenever He wants to, however He wants to do it, yet Him choosing you for such a task, should be humbling. Humbling because God is trusting you with an assignment. An assignment to use the gifts, skills, and talents that He has given you to edify the kingdom. Matthew 6:33 says, "But seek first His kingdom and His righteousness, and all these things (i.e., 'stuff,' success) will be given to you as well." Your assignment is to use the gifts, skills, and talents that He has given you to be a favor demonstrator in the earth realm for His glory. Your assignment is to use the gifts, skills, and talents that He has given you as a testimony of His goodness. God is Sovereign and *God*-success only comes from yielding to His will and walking, by faith, in the purpose that He has ordained for your life. Now, why He chose to use someone like me *still* baffles me. After all that I have done. And trust me, He knows it *all*. Yet, He *still* gives me His peace to persevere. His peace to stand still and His peace to walk in His undeserved grace.

After continuing to allow the words of this song to minister to my spirit, the words took on a whole different meaning. It is this *God*-success which gives you

Little Pearls of Wisdom...The Grace Chronicles

an attitude of servitude; giving you a heart to serve His people. It is this *God*-success which allows you the opportunity to use the gifts that He has given you to help others. It is this *God*-success which allows you to be compassionate and relatable to those in need. This was the unspoken language that my grandmother was showing me. FYI: Do not despise the small subtle lessons. For it is these lessons that can be the premise to you doing something so extraordinary.

#TeamILoveWearingGrandmama'sPearls

You Can Dress It Up However You Want, Sin Is *Still* Sin...

I realize God has treated me with undeserved grace, and so I tell each of you not to think you are better than you really are. Use good sense and measure yourself by the amount of faith that God has given you...Romans 12:3

Patience...

If you had to take a self-evaluation, out of all the fruit of the Spirit, which one would you say you struggle with the most? Be honest. There is no right or wrong answer. This is a time of self-reflection, transparency, and truth. Would you rather call yourself to the carpet, or would you rather God, do it? I will take the former for $300 Alex. So, I will go first. I am not going to sit up here and tell you that manifesting, or walking in, the fruit of the Spirit just comes naturally. It does not. The flesh, my flesh, is sinful and wants to do *all* things contrary to the spirit. Even on my best days, when I think I am 'winning,' my flesh is *still* hard to restrain. I heard something the other day that blessed me and I would

Little Pearls of Wisdom...The Grace Chronicles

like to share it with you if I may. I was listening to an old sermon of my pastor's, and he was talking about this very issue. However, I had never heard it from the perspective that he was preaching it from. The referencing scripture came from Galatians 2:20, "I have been crucified with Christ; it is no longer I who live, but Christ lives in me; and the life which I now live in the flesh I live by faith in the Son of God, who loved me and gave Himself for me." This entire verse is relevant, however, the first six words of this scripture, 'I have been crucified with Christ,' stopped me in my tracks. it. When Paul was writing this epistle, he was not literally saying that he had been crucified with Christ. For we all know that Paul was called to be an Apostle after Jesus' resurrection and ascension into heaven. So, that is not what he meant. Let me ask you a question. What was the underlying purpose Jesus went to the cross? To redeem us from 'our' sins; not His sin, but ours. He paid the price for us to be reconciled back into a relationship with God, The Father. Now, what was the purpose of Jesus being resurrected from death? To show His 'conquering' ability. Jesus showed death, and the enemy, that nothing nor no one could defeat Him. He has all power is in His hands. In knowing this, Jesus has done all the 'heavy lifting' for us. So, what is our part in all of this? By faith, say your 'ABC's' — **a**ccepting, **b**elieving, and **c**onfessing Jesus as your Lord as Savior (Romans 10:9). This is the one and only way that you will have eternal life. Now, that was pretty short and sweet, but anytime I can offer Christ to you, I am jumping at the opportunity. Plus, I just want to ensure that we are all starting from the same level foundation.

Getting back to those six little words, I really began to contemplate this in my spirit. When Paul says that he was crucified with Christ, he was meaning was that his 'old' self (i.e., his sinful nature/flesh) had been crucified/killed with Christ as well. And, when Christ rose 'anew' from the dead, Paul did also. Hence the scripture in 2 Corinthians 5:17, which says, "Therefore if any man be in Christ, he is a new creature: old things are passed away; behold, all things are become new." The only way that you can become 'new' in Christ is if you nail to the cross the 'old' you; figuratively speaking. It is not your flesh that is becoming 'new,' so do not expect to see this new physical version of you in the reflection. If you had freckles before you accepted Christ, then you will still have freckles after you accept Christ. It is not the physical aspect of you that changes, it is the awakening of the spiritual being within you, that now becomes 'new,' or in today's lingo, 'woke.' It is this crucifying of the 'old,' that enables you to now live by the Holy Spirit. Thereby living a life that is *not* your own. A life in which *desires* to manifest the fruit of the Spirit living in you.

Now to answer the original question, the fruit of the Spirit that I struggle the most with is probably patience. Unlike some of the other fruits, patience is one that has to be developed. Seeing the fruit of patience does not manifest quickly nor does it happen overnight. Patience is a process, an on-going process. Which brings me to an experience I once had on the job. Before getting into that experience, allow me to introduce my first little *pearl* of wisdom: "Never get to a point in life where you think that you have anything left to learn. There will always be some form of CE (continuing education) training, to embrace. There is room for improvement in all of us. Once you make yourself 'unavailable' to learn, that is when you stop growing. That is when stagnancy becomes evident."

    A few years ago, I worked at a job where the environment had very laxed boundaries as if there were none in place. And, because of the unrestraint of employee actions, there was always tension. This, in turn, created an environment of extremely low morale. The elephant in the room went unaddressed by upper management and as a result, issues were slowly escalating. Being the newest employee hired, I was in awe at the level of *blasé*-ness that was being tolerated. We are healthcare professionals in a highly trusted profession. And the one thing you never want to do is compromise a patient's health because of unresolved issues happening behind-the-scenes. Not that that ever happened, but when the patients can tell that something is off, it is past the time for having a round table discussion. Well, like I said, I was the

You Can Dress It Up However You Want, Sin Is Still Sin...

most recently hired, therefore, I just kind of sat back, watched, and listened as all this internal friction was going on behind the scenes. This issue had went on for months. And honestly, I began to notice why the elephant in the room was not being addressed. It was because upper management were the ones feeding it. Again, me being shy and reserved by nature, was speechless. That is, until one day while in a meeting, to my surprise, that shy and reserved person left the building. I had had it up to 'here' with the childish, immature, and petty antics, and everyone was going to know about it that day. Once I opened my mouth, the words just would not stop escaping. Not only was I surprised but imagine the elephant feeders. I knew that was going to be my last day. After the meeting was dismissed, as opposed to the tension that hovered over the job, there was an eerie silence. Although what I said may have been the truth, since my presentation was as it was, that could potentially have stopped them from receiving it. My mama used to always tell us as kids, "It's not what you say, it's how you say it." Man, where was mama that day. I wished she were there to put her hand over my mouth because I let my flesh get the best of me. I let my im-patience get the best of me. I let my inappropriateness get the best of me. I did not keep my flesh nailed to the cross! Why did I have a 'spill out?' And why did I feel the need to have to address this issue? I found out two important things that day: 1) My flesh was like a beast unleashed that day. So, I understand why you need to crucify it. I never really thought about the correlation between being *im*-patient and my sinful nature. But I found out that day! There is nothing like having a front row seat to a movie in which you are headlining. And 2) I should have been eating PB&J sandwiches in these meetings. At least that way, I know the peanut butter would have made it hard to talk. LOL.

Even though the meeting was over, the consequences of my actions, were still there. No, I did not get fired, but I was very disappointed in how I had handled myself, as a professional, but even more so as a Christian. My second little pearl of wisdom is: "Do not always look at the results of a person's actions, look at the *why* they did the action. This is what will help alleviate the further repeating of the action."

As I began contemplating my actions, the Holy Spirit showed me something so revelatory. He showed me how if *im*-patience is not crucified (i.e., nailed to the cross), it can lead to sin. Yikes. Allow me to explain. Being *im*-patient is what manifests; what we dress up. But, if I am being completely transparent, the underlying root to why we do not want to wait is because of self; self-gratification (i.e., pride) to name it exactly. Flesh. Sinful nature. We may not want to admit it, but we are narcissistic in our ways. We do not want, nor like, to wait. We do what we want. We want what we

You Can Dress It Up However You Want, Sin Is Still Sin...

want, when we want it, how we want it, as long as we want it. Period. Do not believe me? Just look around. The jail system is full of folks who did not feel the need to have to wait. So, in satisfying their flesh, they acted. Acted trying to satisfy a craving deep within. They acted, trying to relieve a quench for something they believed they wanted. They acted, trying to get a jump on something they believed to be rewarding. They presumptuously gave into a craving to appease their flesh. And guess what? It cost them. So, my next little *pearl* of wisdom is: "Not crucifying the 'old' sinful ways of your flesh to the cross, will cost you as well."

When I mentioned earlier that being *im*-patient is what we dress up, but it is the flesh that is the driving force, this is why Christ was crucified. As you crucify your flesh and nail it to the cross, you are surrendering your will to God, which means that you surrender whatever you had in mind for your life, your expectations, your goals, your plans. As you crucify your flesh and nail it to the cross, you are surrendering your way to God, which means you cannot always respond like you want to respond. No, you cannot always say what you want to say. No, you cannot always do what you want to do. And no, you cannot always go where you want to go. Is this easier said than done? Sure, it is. The struggle was real, then, and the struggle is still real, today. Paul talks about it in Romans 7:17-21, "So I am not the one doing wrong; it is sin living in me that does it. And I know that nothing good lives in me, that is, in my sinful nature. I want to do what is right, but I cannot. I want to do what is good, but I do not. I do not want to do what is wrong, but I do it anyway. But if I do what I do not want to do, I am not really the one doing wrong; it is sin living in me that does it." Will we struggle in our flesh? Absolutely. But should we stay down when we fall prey into our flesh? Girl, no. Get up, fix your crown of grace, pick up your little *pearls* of wisdom, and keep it moving. There is a freedom and liberty in serving Christ, but do not use your freedom to indulge in your flesh (Galatians 5:13). And know that there is no struggle too big that Christ did not nail to that cross!

During this season of my life, I know that God is doing a new thing. He is maturing me, and I know this because I am being stretched. Stretched from my areas of my comfort to areas of extreme uncomfortability. My intentions are being stretched. My integrity is being stretched. My accountability is being stretched. My transparency is being stretched. And, even though I may not have scored too high on that earlier 'elephant in the room' spill out, God is *still* long-suffering with me because as you can tell, I am still on the Potter's wheel.

#TeamLovingTheSmellOf'Newness'

It's Not What You're Called, It's What You *Answer* To...

Remind them to be submissive to rulers and authorities, to obey, to be ready for every good work, to slander no one, to avoid fighting, and to be kind, always showing gentleness to all people... Titus 3:1-3

Kindness...

It never ceases to amaze me how God uses the least likely to accomplish some of His greatest assignments. If I had to name a few, outside of myself of course, I think I would have to start with Mary. Mary was a young virgin girl whom God chose to bring forth His Son, Jesus. That's settles it right there. But, to drive my point, I will go ahead and name just a few more. There was a farmer, whom God used to be one of His mouthpieces. What was unique about this prophet, was that he did not speak out God's prophetic Words, he mimed them. His name was Ezekiel. There was this poetry writing, instrument playing shepherd, who was tending his father's sheep. God sent His prophet Jeremiah to anoint this young boy. This young boy went on to become one of Israel's greatest kings, who was also a man after God's own heart. This king's name was David. There was a woman prophetess, who happens to be the only female judge mentioned in the Bible, who was a great warrior. God used her to kill an army of nine hundred. Her name was Deborah. There was this infamous persecutor of Christians, turned apostle, whom God used to write the majority of the New Testament; by bringing forth Christ's message of the Good News. This notorious man's name was Paul. And then there was Moses. The 'least likely' where I am going to stick my pin. Moses was an orphaned child who had very humble beginnings. But God chose him to handle such great responsibilities that you can read all about in the Book of Exodus. In everything that God instructed Moses to do, every miracle he performed, God equipped him. With all that Moses did, it was something that God told him, that just kept ringing in my spirit. Real briefly, God instructed Moses to go to Pharaoh, in Egypt, with this command in Exodus 3:10, "Now go, for I am sending you to Pharaoh. You must lead my people Israel out of Egypt." Moses was, of course, very apprehensive about this grave assignment because he was looking at his ability, and not the ability of the

It's Not What You're Called, It's What You Answer To...

God who was sending him. My first little *pearl* of wisdom, "When God tells you to go, 'Go.' Obedience is much better than the sacrifice." When Moses asked God, "Whom shall I say sent me," it was God's response that I could not stop contemplating. It is found in Exodus 3:14, "God replied to Moses, 'I AM WHO I AM.'" Do you realize just how 'Boss' that statement is? Man, this was like God giving Moses a blank check! You know how checks have that line that says, "Pay to the order of?" Well, on that line, God's response was left blank. Not because God had forgotten to write something there, but because He was giving Moses (i.e., you and me), the power, permission, and authority to fill it in. And whatever is written on the line, God says, "I got you! You need that, I Am _____. You want that, I Am _____. There is nothing that you can put on that line that I Am not." That is a real Boss move from Sovereign God who has an unlimited supply! Wait for it. Wait for it. Wait for it. If God gave Moses a blank check, what do you think that means for you and for me? I Am have given us a blank check! I do not know about you, but I am going to use my writing authority!

I just gave some examples of how God can use the least likely to do great works. Let's shift gears here for a minute. Same God. Different 'least likely' candidates. God's glory still being revealed. During the time that these Bible narratives were being recorded, not only were the laws a lot stricter than they are today, but the punishments were more cruel and harsher as well. And one of the most common punishments was stoning. Maybe some of the offenders who were punished by this method, deserved it because of the violation of the law that they committed. That is neither here nor there. From the stories that I have read, whether the 'offender' was innocent or guilty, was not the bigger message to be learned. The message that Jesus wanted every to receive was to not judge your brother/sister, but to show grace and compassion towards them. To share the gift of kindness with them, the way that God has shared with you.

    Let me share with you a little insight that the Holy Spirit shared with me. In both of these illustrations, two remarkable women are involved. I just want you to take note of how God's kindness blots out the offense of the accused and His grace reigns Supreme. Christ's response is how we, as Believers/Disciples/Ambassadors for Christ, should be towards one another. The first demonstration of God's grace and kindness can be found in John 8:3-11. Many of us may be familiar with the story of the woman who was *caught* in the act of adultery. This woman was not only caught, but she was publicly *exposed* in front of her peers. Notice, I did say that she was *caught*, not implied. *Caught*, not assumed. *Caught*, not presumed. This woman was *caught* in her sin. Now,

It's Not What You're Called, It's What You Answer To...

please do not misunderstand what I am about to say next. Take it with a grain of salt and let's continue moving on. Some may agree, or disagree, but in today's society, adultery does not carry the charge, or the weight, like it did in this woman's time. Today, in my opinion, it has been extremely watered down and presumably more acceptable. Hence, terms like side-chick, sidepiece, my boo-thang, my #2, mistress, 'drop it like it's hot girl', 'shadows girl', my 'hit-it-n-quit-it' girl, or the like. It is almost a glorified position to be in if this is your role. However, this is not how it was in those times. This woman was living in a male dominated, misogynistic society. Being an adulterer, for a woman, was a position of disgrace and dishonor. And, if found in this position, the punishment was typically death by stoning. We do not see any of that going on in today's society. It is almost normal to see a married couple who live separate lives. Sometimes even while living under the same roof. I do not exactly when, but somewhere along the lines, the institute of marriage has compromised its vows, not just to the two individuals involved, but to God. There is little allegiance, or loyalty, to the sanctity of marriage. People want the glitz and glamour of telling of their *fairy tale* wedding. But, many are not willing to 'get down and dirty' and fight for the marriage, when all the glitz and glamour have left the building. The one thing I was taught as a little girl was that anything worth having is worth fighting for. Whether it is going to school, keeping a job, fighting for a relationship, or working towards a goal. If something is worth it to you, you will fight for it. Alright, I am done. I am off my soapbox for now. But getting back to this particularly interesting woman. This woman, in those times, was not allowed to have a voice. And, because she did not have a voice, she was looked upon as being the lowest of the low. A lower-class citizen with no rights. She had no substantial value; or any value at all for that matter. I am hoping you are grasping the times that this woman was living in. People always argue that they would have been rebellious and would have had a tough time adapting to the ways of the times. Some may have. However, I beg to differ just a little bit because if this were all you knew, if this were all you had been exposed to, if this were all you had ever seen, I do not know how much rebelling would be going on. This was the custom of those days and if you were the one to make waves, then I am sure you would have paid for it with your life. Certain behavior was just not tolerated; especially not coming from a woman. The rules and the expectations were pretty cut and dry and I need you to understand this story from this woman's perspective, so that you will be able to catch the revelation that I was shown.

    Now, before we get into the meat of this story, I am sure some may have a few questions. Questions like, "If this woman was *caught* in the act, who was she *caught* with? The other guilty party was never even mentioned. Like she was *caught* by herself or something. Almost like the identity of her ghost co-conspirator was irrelevant. Do not forget, remember the times. The only detail that was given as a 'need to know' basis is that she, all by her lonesome self, was the offender. The *only* guilty party being accused. And get this. The text never once mentioned if she, or her ghost co-conspirator, was the married party. If she was married, where was her husband in all of this? Who caught her? You are following nicely. The scripture says in verse 3, that the teachers of the Law and the Pharisees are the ones who brought her in. Now, wait a minute. This woman was *caught* in the act, right? How did the Law teachers and the Pharisees thus catch her? Were they there watching her? Where did they come from? Why were not they in the temple honoring the position that they were called to do — teach! Here is my first little pearl of wisdom for you: Sometimes it is the people closest to you that are plotting against you. Just because folks smile in your face does not mean that they want to see you succeed and prosper. And someone may be waiting in the cut, for you to slip up and fall, so that they can accuse you too. Now, that was free! Do with it what you want. But somebody may have needed to hear that. Now, back to our regularly scheduled program. This particularly interesting woman was the only one, in this duo equation, who had her shame and guilt exposed. It takes two to tango, right? So, in my opinion, it does not matter the role she played in this act, she did it. Own it and take the charge. My only problem is that she was the only one. Her ghost co-conspirator should have been exposed, humiliated, and disciplined publicly as well. And, if I am not mistaken, doesn't it take two people to commit adultery? If he was the married one, then it was him who violated the vows he made to his wife. It was him who stepped out of his covenantal marriage. It was him who wanted to have his cake and eat it too. Why was his responsibility in this whole ordeal overlooked? Not addressed? Swept under the rug? He was never held to be accountable for his actions, unlike this woman. Nonetheless, the total responsibility of the offense fell all on her. What should have been good for the goose should have been good for the gander. That is obviously *not* a true saying.

As you can tell, I can be very opinionated about certain things, so I say this next statement solely as my own. Remember family, this is a judge-free zone. From the beginning, women were built to be Tonka tough. We have had to accept less when we know we deserve more. We have had to be silent, and go unnoticed, because women were meant to be discreet and should be seen and not heard. We have had to sometimes compromise, or 'dumb' down, our knowledge base or skill set to make others not feel intimidated or insecure about our intelligence. So yes, women have always had to be silent warriors. And it is from this type of endurance that keeps us evolving into these mighty, tenacious, passionate, and powerful prayer warriors that we are today. So, 'Thank you' to all those things that tried to hold me down. 'Thank you' to all those things that tried to keep a foot in my back. 'Thank you' to all those things that tried to choke the life out of me. 'Thank you' to all those things that tried to keep me from hearing; that tried to keep me from seeing. 'Thank you' to all those things that tried to make me run and hide like a girl. So, what if I ran. I just did not run to where you may have thought. I ran to get on my knees. I ran to my Daddy (i.e., God). Because if I do not know anything else, I know that God *always* has my back. Man, my Daddy is kind. He is full of grace. And I know that my Daddy loves me; no matter what. God loves me so much that He *gave,* so that I could *have* (For God so loved the world that He gave His one and only Son, that whoever believes in Him shall not perish but have eternal life; John 3:16). God loves me so much that He fights my battles for me (2 Chronicles 20:15). God loves me so much that He has given me victory over the enemy through the process (Genesis 3:15). Period.

All right. I may have gotten a little off-track, but

now for real. Back to our regularly scheduled program concerning this outcasted, publicly humiliated, guilt-shamed, but extremely brave woman. It is one thing when you have been accused, and you did not do what they said you did. But it is a whole different ball game when you have been accused, and you actually did do what they say you did. How do you deal with that? How do you walk, with your head held high, not letting your crown of grace tilt off your head, past those same folks that you know are your accusers? How do you look at yourself in the mirror? How do you deal with the embarrassment? The guilt? The shame? Well, I am glad you asked because this has been a place where I have received my mail before. And, I was shown a *perfect* example, found in a *perfect* Word, demonstrated by a *perfect* Man. I have not deviated from the previous text. I am still in the scripture dealing with this adulterous woman. Watch this. The crowd that this woman was exposed in front of, were chanting, "Stone her. Stone her. She should die for what she has done. She does not deserve another chance. Stone her." It has always baffled me the amount of fury they had for this one woman. It was like what she had done had offended them or something. But why was there such an underlying anger for the action she committed? Of course, I am going to offer some different perspectives to think about, which may differ from yours. Just stay open. As far as

It's Not What You're Called, It's What You Answer To...

the onlookers' anger towards this woman, one of my thought processes was that maybe the accusers were so condemning because they saw a little bit of themselves in what she was being accused of. Skating the lines of being a hypocrite. You know throwing the rock and hiding your hand kind of thing. It never ceases to amaze me how some folks can be harder on others that are caught, knowing all the while that they have been doing the same thing as the accused. My second little *pearl* of wisdom is to be mindful of folks who condemn so easily. They may be disguising, like they are condemning the action, but they may just be trying to create a stir in order to keep the focus off them. What they have been doing in the dark is still in the dark; which sometimes gives a self-righteousness to be judgmental and condemning; all because the spotlight has not caught up with them yet. Bottom line: The only difference between this woman and her accusers, is that she was exposed in her sin, and they were still hiding in theirs. I am so glad that her fate, as well as ours, is not in the hands of man. But that our fate is in the hands of a forgiving, kind, and compassionate God. I am so glad that when man only looks at our actions, it is God who looks at the heart and the intent. I am so glad that man's judgment does not determine how God sees me or even what He calls me. When everyone was ready to condemn this woman, God's kindness, demonstrated through the hands of

Jesus Christ, stepped in, and overrode their system. Psst...They did not understand that when Jesus steps on the scene, He is the System that overrides all systems. In this woman's condemnation, Christ's kindness forgave her. Christ's kindness covered her. His kindness protected her and shielded her. But, above all, it does not matter that she did what they said she did, it never changed the love that Christ showed her. He loved her through her imperfections. He loved her through her insecurities. He loved her through her flaws. He even loved her through her mistakes. This quiet sermon that Christ demonstrated as he stooped (verse 6), was so impactful and thunderous that when He looked up, there would be no one left to accuse her. Cannot nobody shut the mouth of your nay-sayers quite like Jesus!

As we *God*-vigate our journey as women, there may be times when our crown gets tilted. In other words, there may be times when our choices take us down a path where we fall a little from grace. As opposed to condemning one another from a place of disgrace or dishonor, we are here to lift one another up. Galatians 6:1 says, "Dear brothers and sisters, if another believer is overcome by some sin, you who are godly should gently and humbly help that person back onto the right path. And be careful not to fall into the same temptation yourself." I believe an important little *pearl* of wisdom to add is that before

It's Not What You're Called, It's What You Answer To...

you go inserting yourself into an equation where you have to squeeze to fit, stop and think. Think about this adulterous woman. Think about her offense. Think about how embarrassed and shameful she must have felt. Think about her anxiety level as the crowd was yelling and screaming at her. Think about her fear as she waited, nervously, for them to throw the stones they had gripped in their hands. But I need you to also think about this. Think about the humility that exuded her in the forgiveness she received. You cannot downplay the compassion that she was given. Do not overshadow the kindness that was shown to her. These are the same little *pearls* that we should be extending to our sisters in their time of need. Only in my mind, I can imagine that as Jesus was standing up from writing on the ground, He was straightening out her crown of grace. Putting it back in its rightful place. When is the last time you straightened out your sister's crown?

Now, the second illustration of God's kindness can be found in Joshua 2. This is the story of Rahab. Keep in mind that women are still viewed the same way as they were in the previous illustration. The premise of this story, however, is that Moses sent Joshua, Caleb, and some other spies, to go out and spy out this occupied land that God had promised them. However, once they reached the territory, to avoid being killed by the inhabitants of the land, they needed shelter.

Little Pearls of Wisdom...The Grace Chronicles

They needed some place to lay low and be out of sight. I got a question for you? Has your reputation ever preceded you? Well, Joshua & Caleb's reputation had preceded them, but in a good way. Because God was on their side and had allowed them to defeat many, other nations were very intimidated by them; including this nation that inhabited the Promised Land. The woman that they had met was an inhabitant of this territory, and she too had heard how God had been fighting their battles. This woman's name was Rahab, and she invited the men to stay at her home, helping to ensure their safety. Now, let me share a little bit about Rahab. Rahab just was not your 'average' woman. Rahab was a 'working' woman. Yes, she was a prostitute. FYI: Again, in this story, God's grace and mercy stooped down. And, in this stooping, God's kindness overshadowed Rahab's missteps, mistakes, detours, or any wrong turns that she made. And ultimately, because of Rahab's actions and reverence for God, she was remembered. And her courage has been recognized as being a heroine. Here is a little *pearl* of wisdom that I am just throwing out there, "It does not matter where you start. It does not matter where you live. It does not matter what you have or do not have. It does not matter what your environment looks like, it is all about how you finish." God can, and will, use *anyone* He wants to use to be a blessing for His purpose. He will even blow your mind and use those whom society has considered to be 'thrown aways' or 'misfits,' all for His glory. As I studied further, the Holy Spirit gave me insight about Rahab's character that I had never considered before. Rahab was a picture of strength, courage, compassion, and kindness. Rahab did not allow her surroundings to dictate her beliefs. Rahab was valuable; even though her environment did not consider her to be nothing more than a prostitute. Rahab acted; even though she knew she was jeopardizing herself and her family's life. Rahab acted; even though her fear was competing with her faith. Rahab acted; even though she may have had to go at it alone. Even though idols were worshiped all throughout the land, Rahab had come to reverence the God of the Israelites because she had 'heard' how He had been protecting them and fighting their battles. And, in Joshua 2:11, she declared the God of the Israelites to be her God, the God of the heavens and the earth. As Rahab intervened to protect those whom she knew were from God, God blessed her. Rahab demonstrated a fear like no other. And, in this moment, her fear pushed her to act in faith; and because of that, the trajectory of her life was never the same. Also, I need you to take note of the compassion and kindness that Rahab demonstrated towards total strangers. Total strangers that she put her life on the line to protect. In Joshua 2:12-14, Rahab states, "Now then, please swear to me by the Lord that, as I have dealt kindly with you, you also will deal kindly with my father's house, and give me a sure sign that you will save alive my father and mother, my brothers and sisters, and all who belong to them, and deliver our lives from death." I believe, whole-heartedly, that one seed of kindness grows another. This becomes evident in verse fourteen when the spies respond, "And the men said to her, 'Our life for yours even to death! If you do not tell this business of ours, then when the Lord gives us the land we will deal kindly and faithfully with you.'" Rahab's one act of kindness not only saved her and her household, but she ended up being in the lineage of Jesus Christ! How is that for not being defined by your past? How is that for God showing kindness to someone who may have thought that she did not deserve it? How is that for your blessing not being predicated on your mistakes? How is that for a little *pearl* of wisdom to be able to walk away with; all from God showing you kindness and showering you with His grace.

    There are many more instances of God giving His impressive grace and kindness to women just like you and me — *perfectly* flawed women. Women who have insecurities and have made mistakes. Women whose crowns have tilted from some left turns and detours. Women who have been vulnerable and who have felt devalued and unloved. But God. The same God of the 'nameless' woman who was caught in the act of adultery, to the protection of Rahab and her family, He is the same yesterday, today, and forevermore (Hebrews 13:8). So, if He did it for them, He is able to do it for you. For me. So, do not just read these stories that the Holy Spirit illuminated as something for your entertainment, or for your enjoyment. They are blueprints to show that God's grace covers all sin; even to those you may not think deserve a second chance.

Do you know what I really admire about these two women? In their deliverance, they never forgot where God found them and what He did for them. My last little *pearl* of wisdom is to encourage you to tell your real testimony. The one that someone is waiting to hear. The one that is going to uplift and encourage another. The one that is going to glorify the Sovereign God that we serve. Besides, who are you trying to impress by 'prettying' up your testimony? Girl, just be transparent and watch God use you to be a blessing to others. I am telling you what I know, and not what I have heard.

In each of their cases, these women were given a second chance. These women were the one(s) who were *not* left behind. These women were the one(s) who were *not* forgotten. These women were the one(s) in which their past did *not* supersede their purpose. These women were the one(s) who experienced an outward demonstration of the grace and kindness of God. The last thing the Holy Spirit showed me about

Little Pearls of Wisdom...The Grace Chronicles

these women, is that they were both, to some degree promiscuous. In order to appreciate what He told me next, allow me to give you a very brief definition of promiscuous. When a person is promiscuous, they are *un*-restricted in their actions. They have no boundaries. No limits. And that is when He said, "God gives promiscuous (*un*-restraint, *limit*-less, indiscriminate, *un*-discriminating) grace to promiscuous women."

#TeamNotSoEasilyBroken

You Have All You Need In *Your* House...
Then she came and told the man of God. And he said, "Go, sell the oil, and pay your debt: and you and your sons live on the rest"...2 Kings 4:7

Goodness...

One of my favorite parables in the Bible is found in the gospels. Although each gospel writes a similar, but different, account of the same parable, for this inference, I am going to reference the one that is found in Matthew 14:13-21. This is the parable when Jesus fed the five thousand (not including women and children), after a day full of teaching and healing the sick. For so long, I only looked at the obvious miracle that Jesus performed — feeding the multitude with only two fish and five loaves of bread. To the natural eye, only have this amount would have been ludicrous to even offer. However, if most are familiar with this parable, you already know that Jesus did His thang! This is what I like to call the *direct* miracle because this was the miracle that was clearly evident. It was visible and seen by those in attendance. However, there was also an implied miracle that I was shown; that is just as relevant as the former. The more I read this parable, the more the Holy Spirit began dealing with me on the *indirect* miracle which took place. For years, I had been taught, and only focused on the obvious *direct* miracle. But I had been missing the *un*-obvious *indirect* miracle. The *indirect* miracle of *not* what was provided in a time of need, but what was actually left over, after the need had been met. And, not just met, but fulfilled and exceeded. This was a crucial part that I had overlooked. Hence, this is where my lesson began.

Again, I love this parable. But there were two verses that just kept stirring in my spirit, Matthew 14, verses 20 & 22. Matthew 14:20 says, "They all ate and were satisfied, and the disciples picked up twelve basketfuls of broken pieces that were left over." By this time, everyone had eaten; all the men, all the women, and all the children alike. Over five thousand in total (verse 21). And verse 22 reads, "Immediately, Jesus made the disciples get into the boat and go on ahead of Him to the other side, while He dismissed the crowd." It was here, when the Holy Spirit began giving me insight that I had never seen before. Let's get this party started!

Jesus tells His disciples to go to the other side. But, for what? What are they supposed to do with the food they picked up? The answer should not be this complicated. Sounds like there should be a common-sense answer, right? Close, but no cigar. This is a place in the crossroads of life, where I know, we have all been; internally struggling with something your senses are telling you to do, but yet, you hear a small still voice telling you to do something that does not make any sense at all. Welcome to your inflection point! It is here where you decide if you are going to lead by your own senses or are you going to surrender what you may have in mind, and allow your sixth sense (i.e., the Holy Spirit) to take the lead on this one. FYI: I called the Holy Spirit the sixth sense only because with all things being equal, most people have five active senses — sense of sight, sense of hearing, sense of touch, sense of taste, and sense of smell. These are the senses that govern us. However, when you allow the Holy Spirit to govern, He is that sixth sense that puts all those other senses to shame because what He tells you to do, does not make any sense. And your other senses are in conflict with what the One Spirit, the Holy Spirit, is leading you to do. It is here, if we are being transparent, that some of us struggle. It is here, if we are being honest, that some of us have a hard time surrendering. However, it is here, where God's plan supersedes anything, you may have had in mind, if you obey. It is also here where the Holy Spirit trumps common sense! The only question is, "Who are you going to allow to lead you?" Mind-blowing! This was the pivotal part that I had been missing. My 'lightbulb moment.'

Getting back to this parable, however, at no time did Jesus give specific instructions to the disciples, as to what to do with the food that they had picked up. He never told them to discard the left-overs. He never even told the disciples to make 'doggy bags' and distribute the remaining fragments of food among the people that were there. Jesus gave quite simple orders to pick up whatever was remaining, get in the boat, and make your way to the other side of the water. And that He would stay behind and disperse the left-over crowd. Did you catch how precise Jesus' instructions were? He told them play-by-play what to do with the fragments. Then the Holy Spirit began to enlighten me on the significance of left-overs. And, not just left-overs as it pertains to this parable but left-overs in general. Hopefully, you will better understand as we continue on this journey. Still with me? Let's keep going...

The more I prayed and meditated, the more I kept hearing in my spirit, "Do not discard the left-overs. Do not discard the left-overs." Before my understanding was broadened, I was only applying that message to this parable. But the Holy Spirit wanted to deposit so much more. This is an important concept, so I will go step-by-step in the same way that it was given to me.

You Have All You Need In Your House...

Because some of us have limited perspective, we only focus on what the disciples had — two fish and five loaves. We look at what we have to start with. Or the lack thereof. However, it is not so much about how you start, but it is how you finish. It is important that you always remember that. Therefore, if you believe that, then it does not matter if you are at the beginning, in the middle, or on the homestretch towards the end, give thanks. God is able to bless your ending before you even start. And He is able to bless your middle when you do not have enough to even start. No matter where you are or what you do not have for the journey, just thank Him for the process!

In this parable, God showed, where He can take a little, and multiply it to much. God did not perform simple addition, He multiplied it! God blew their minds with this immediate blessing. A blessing so big that when He opened the floodgates of heaven, and poured it out, they did not have room enough to receive (Malachi 3:10). Hence the left-overs. God blessed them so abundantly that the excess of the left-overs went unnoticed (i.e., the *indirect* miracle). God blessed them so abundantly that they had more food left over than what they started with! Twelve baskets over! Now, this is just me. So, you can agree to disagree. But I believe that since there were twelve disciples and there were also twelve baskets left over, each disciple was able to carry their own basket away as evidence. Evidence of the miracle that they had just seen and witnessed. Evidence of the miracle that God is able to do exceedingly, abundantly, above all that we can ever ask or think (Ephesians 3:20). Evidence of the miracle that God is able to supply all of your needs according to His riches in glory (Philippians 4:19). Not your riches, your neighbor's riches, or your boo's riches, but His riches! His, and His alone. Oh, what an awesome God we serve! The mic has just been dropped!

    Getting back to what I kept hearing, "Do not discard the left-overs. Do not discard the left-overs." Although these were the instructions that Jesus gave His disciples, this was very closely related to what I had been experiencing within the past couple of years. Still walking with me? All right. We have all been privy to this pandemic, which infiltrated, infected, and inflicted too many lives to count. However, many did not know that I, too, had been dealing with my own personal little pandemic. The same way COVID-19 left the world in a state of bafflement, uncertainty, and fearfulness, so did my own personal little pandemic — separation from my husband. I do not like to keep harping on what I have been through, but it is necessary. You cannot appreciate where I am now if you do not know where I came from. I'm trying to show you that I am a living, walking testimony of Isaiah 61: 3, "To appoint unto them that mourn in Zion, to give unto them beauty for ashes, the oil of joy for mourning, the garment of praise for the spirit of heaviness; that they might be called trees of righteousness, the planting of the Lord, that He might be glorified." God raised me up, lifted my heaviness, gave me some new clothes, and a praise on my lips. The enemy thought he had me, but God. God used my pain to push me into my purpose. And my life has yet to be the same. So, my first little *pearl* of wisdom is to not be intimidated by life's uncertainties. Do not be intimidated if you have to stand by yourself (although we are never alone; Joshua 1:9). And do not be intimidated by the troubles you face. I would love to be able to take the credit for this next statement, but I cannot. One of my instructors said it while we were in class one day, and I have never forgotten it. You *can* take this statement to the bank, "There is treasure hidden beneath your pain." We all have had our fair share of struggles and disappointments, but God promises that nothing you have been through, will be wasted. This left-over illustration is double-sided. The first side is regarding your life experiences. Everything that you have been through, God is able to use. Even if you do not think it is valuable, watch God use it for His glory. The other side of this word left-overs, pertains to us, as people. I can only speak for myself, but there have been times in my life where folks counted me out and wanted to discard of me. But God did not let that happen. The same way that I am a left-over, I refuse to discard the left-overs that have helped me to evolve into the woman that I am today. So, instead of looking at my separation as something to regret, I looked at it as an opportunity. An opportunity that was necessary. Necessary for my growth. Necessary for my purpose. Necessary for my destiny. Necessary for the testimony that I would give of God's goodness shown towards me. If I had not gone through all that I went through, I would have probably discarded my left-overs, myself included. I am not a hoarder, but I do not discard of nuttin.' My left-overs are my evidence. My left-overs are a reminder of what God *can* do. My left-overs are a reminder of where God brought me from. My left-overs represent how God took the little that I had and multiplied it for His glory. My left-overs tell my story about how God is a delivering God. And, how He brought me through. My left-overs tell my story about how God is a providing God. And, in the midst of confusion and uncertainty, in the midst of 'not enough,' in the midst of sickness and *dis*-ease, in the midst of lack and disaster, God made a way. The left-overs tell my whole story. My transparent story about how God is a God that is all-loving and never-failing.

    I know it may be a little hard to embrace the extent of the season that I was in. Even though I was in a season of despair, God never once let me look how I may have felt on the inside. He allowed me to not just come out of that season, not looking like what I had been through, but He allowed me to come out with more than what I went in with. I came out with a basketful of left-overs! Which leads me to my second little pearl of wisdom — trust God. Do not look at what you do not have, trust God. Do not look at who is not with you, trust God. Do not look at your circumstances, trust God. Trust God. Trust God. Trust Him. I cannot say it enough. When I could not rely, or depend, on anyone or anything, including myself, God *never* stopped being good. When I was not good, God *never* stopped being good. When things around me were not good, God *never* stopped being good. One more time for the road — God *never* stopped being good. Want to know why? Because God is faithful, and He loves us! Period. Psalm 17:8-9 says it best, "Keep me as the apple of your eye; hide me in the shadow of your wings from the wicked who are out to destroy me, from my mortal enemies who surround me." You may not be the apple of nobody else's eye, but isn't it good to know that you are the apple of His?

Here is my last little *pearl* of wisdom for you to keep close — No matter what you are up against, allow me to leave you with these five little words — God has gotten you covered. Now is not the time to be quitting. Now is not the time to be giving up. Now is not the time to take for granted the second chance(s) that you have been given. Someone is waiting to hear about that basketful you have been carrying around, with your fragments in it. And I know you have fragments sis, so share them! Where so many suffered loss during this season that we are all in, God's goodness sustained you. Just look down at your basketfuls! The basketful of left-overs are your testimony. The basketful of left-overs represent God's provision during these uncertain times. The basketful of left-overs should remind you that God has got you. The basketful of left-overs is a perfect demonstration of how God can use the little that you think you have and multiply it beyond measure; all for His glory. Thank Him for the little and watch Him increase you beyond anything your mind could ever conceive (Matthew 14:19)!

#TeamDoNotOverlookTheSmallThings

God Covers *All* Of Our Short-Comings...
Brothers and sisters, I do not consider that I have made it my own yet; but one thing I do: forgetting what lies behind and reaching forward to what lies ahead, I press on toward the goal to win the heavenly prize of the upward call of God in Christ Jesus...Philippians 3:13-14

Faithfulness...

Hi again. It's still me, Tena. Did I mention that I am perfectly flawed? I know you have heard me talk about this in an earlier chapter, but for some reason, I am being led to reiterate it. I know that the Bible tells us to crucify our flesh, but let's be real, that is sometimes a little easier said than done. I also know that Romans 6:6 says, "We know that our old sinful selves were crucified with Christ so that sin might lose its power in our lives. We are no longer slaves to sin." Did you hear the words that I just wrote on this paper? It says that being bound to sin makes us slaves! Who, voluntarily, wants to be a slave? Our sin nature (i.e., flesh) gives us permission to do, but what Christ did was give us permission not to do. Christ redeemed us from this bondage, yet some of us *still* walk right back into it. Is that crazy or nah? Since I am all about being *fully* transparent, and this is a safe space, I feel comfortable saying that I used to struggle in this area; quite frequently. Do not look at what you see now, you should have known me then. Then maybe you would understand my testimony! But since you were not there, I dare not leave out any little detail. This is one of the reasons why it is hard for me to be judgmental. Because I know the *real* place I was at, when I cried out to God. Therefore, I am no different from anyone else. God is still working in me, through me, and on me! Selah.

There was a time when all I thought about was 'living my best life,' whatever that meant. And, truth be told, I enjoyed it. I liked reminiscing with that 'old' version of me. I enjoyed the times when I felt the need to 'catch up' and talk about what has been going on with her lately. Can I tell you a secret? I liked to seek her advice because I knew she was going to tell me something that I wanted to hear. I knew she was going to stroke my ego. However, the only time that 'old' her became a problem was when she got too greedy, and she wanted to control every aspect of my life. She wanted to take over things when I did not want, or asked, her too. But did she listen? No

God Covers All Of Our Short-Comings...

ma'am Pam! She craved what she craved and wanted what she wanted. Period. So, when she would get in 'that' mood and wanted to take over the scene, who was really to blame? No one except that precious little face staring back at me in the mirror, 'Me.' Have you heard the saying, "Give an inch and they'll take a yard?" Ding, ding, ding. That was her. That was my flesh. That is 'old' girl. She is like the little Energizer bunny; she just keeps going and going and going. Never being full. Never being satisfied. Never being satiated. I was starting to understand why she needed to be crucified. I teeter-tottered for a while before I really understood that flesh equals sin. Sin equals separation. And separation from God equals death. Plain and simple. Cut and dry. So, why was it so hard for me to 'cut the cord' of my flesh at times? What was my problem? Do you recall me talking about our five senses in the previous chapter? Well, there lies part of the problem. Hear me out. Before we were physical beings, we were spirit beings. Two different systems. Two different lifelines. When God created you, and you became physical, you became part of the world and the world relies on things you can see, hear, feel, touch and smell. Do you follow me? These are the senses that help you navigate your way in the natural and physical world. However, since we are spiritual beings having a natural and physical experience, we have the advantage of being able to rely on both systems — physical and spiritual. In the physical world, you are governed by your flesh and your five senses. However, in the spiritual realm, you are governed by your spirit, being led by the Holy Spirit. In the physical, your five senses can only take you so far. But, in the spiritual, the Holy Spirit knows the thoughts of God (1 Corinthians 2:11) and searched our hearts (Romans 8:27). Therefore, being in a physical body, but allowing our spirit to be led by the Holy Spirit, is almost like we are cheating at this game of life. All because God has given us an advantage. Even an advantage over sin. Sin which comes from our flesh and sin which comes from the source of the sin in our flesh — the enemy. Now, this becomes a problem to those who do not believe. I am not here to debate that. I am only here to share the things that have been shared with me. Take it or leave it.

  Anyone that knows me, knows that one of the ways that I like to decompress is by watching television. I like to watch what I like to call 'mush' tv. My profession requires me to always have my brain turned 'on.' So, when I get home, I like to decompress with shows that allow my brain to just turn 'off' and take a break. Hence, the name 'mush' tv. So, to watch a television preacher is certainly not my idea of 'mush' tv. Both of my grandparents used to watch TBN and the sort all day long. And I used to wonder why they would torcher themselves like that. I did not understand what they

God Covers All Of Our Short-Comings...

could possibly be getting out of watching a tv minister. I used to think that there was nothing like fellowshipping inside a church building. But look at where we have come from. The pandemic has changed a lot of what we used to consider the 'norm.' So, like many, if you were hungry, you had to find another way to eat. Something happened to me yall within the past few years, I have not been able to push away from the table; God's table that is (His written Word). So, my first little *pearl* of wisdom is to never say what you will never do. All I can do is sit back and laugh when I think about how hard of a time, I would give my grandparents for doing what I am doing now. God has a funny way of increasing your appetite!

So, I have added watching ministry television to my 'mush' tv repertoire. As I was watching one night, I caught one of the sermons right in the middle; exactly where I needed to be tuned in. The referencing scripture was 2 Kings 6:17-20. One of the verses that just kept resonating in my belly was verse seventeen, "And Elisha prayed, 'Open his eyes, Lord, so that he may see.' Then the Lord opened the servant's eyes, and he looked and saw the hills full of horses and chariots of fire all around Elisha." The elementary message of the minister was so impactful, "Open your eyes. Everything that you need, you have. All that you need, you have. You are never alone because God will never leave you to manage things alone. We have access to all of heaven's resources, we just need to take advantage of it." Then, the minister advised the listening audience to do something that I had never done before. He instructed us to call forth our angels. He said to call on our angels just to abide and dwell with us. Angels to cover our bodies. Angels to encamp around our beds. Angels to stand post around our homes. Angels to carry us as we drive our vehicles. I have quoted this scripture, with boldness and confidence, in the past, yet, the Holy Spirit gave me a whole different perspective, or insight, as it all collided with this sermon. I could no longer blame God and expect Him to do all of the work. I had to do something. I had to open my mouth. I had to activate my own faith. I had to do my part, in the natural, and allow Him to do His part, in the super. The reality check was that whatever I lacked, it was not because God could not provide. If I had not, it was because I asked not (James 4:3). Honestly, I did not know that there are bands of angels, at our disposal, all around us to cover and protect us (Psalm 91:11). But, once I got this revelation down in my spirit, ya' girl began asking! I immediately began praying and calling forth my angels to cover my mind, my home, my finances, my health. I commanded my angels to protect my family, my child, my job, my friends. Whatever was in my spirit, I uttered until I got a release. Once I did, I wrapped up my prayer and went about my day.

God Covers All Of Our Short-Comings...

Later on, that same night, something out of the ordinary happened. Before I was just about to get into that good REM sleep, my rest was abruptly interrupted by this loud thumping noise. To this day, I cannot tell you what that noise was that woke me up. But I can tell you that if I had to guess, it sounded like someone had slammed up against my front door. Because of this obnoxious and sudden sound, startlement was the first thing I felt when I awoke. Anyone that knows me knows that I do not like being afraid for three main reasons: 1) I live alone. And, if I ever had any concerns about living alone, it is that someone else, who possibly could be watching me, also knows that I live alone. 2) The way that my apartment is positioned is peculiar. It is situated in a nook. So, if anyone chooses to visit, their coming by is intentional because I am the only apartment tucked away in that corner. And 3) People are kidnapping little girls that look like me. LOL. That is similar to a line from the movie The Benchwarmers with Rob Schneider and Nick Swardson. But seriously. I also do not engage in watching scary or suspenseful-type movies for the same reason. So, after hearing the noise, I immediately tried to convince myself that maybe I did not actually hear what I thought I had heard. However, no matter how hard I tried to forget about what had just happened, there were two witnesses that agreed with me that something did, in fact, happen. My two yorkies were my witnesses. They were asleep in the living room and the noise startled them as well and sent them into a barking uproar. About 20-30 minutes later of trying to calm all of us down, as I was lying in bed, the reflection of red and blue lights was flashing through my bedroom windows. This was not a normal occurrence. So of course, I got up to investigate. As I began looking out of the window, I noticed a slew of police cars, at least six or seven, parked right outside of my building. To this day, I still do not know the details of all that had happened that night. But my Spidey sense told me that they were looking for either someone or something, or both. I had never seen so many streams of flashlights glaring at one time. Up. Down. Right. Left. Backwards. Forward. There was not a spot that was off limits from getting exposed. Still intrigued, however, by this out-of-the-ordinary occurrence, I grabbed a seat in my window seal and watched them for a moment. As I was watching all this happen outside, there was an out-of-the-ordinary event that was beginning to happen, to me, on the inside. I was unctioned to start praying. Praying for the families of those who have taken a civil pledge to protect our freedom. Praying for their safety, their protection, their guidance, their endurance, and their mental faculties to be able to deliver justice properly. I was just praying. Now, one of the routine prayers that I pray is, "Lord, protect me from dangers seen and

God Covers All Of Our Short-Comings...

unseen." As I was praying for the civil servicemen, this simple little prayer was brought back to my remembrance. And, what the Holy Spirit showed me was the power in my words. When you ask in faith and believe in your heart, you can ask what you will, and it shall be given unto you (Matthew 21:22). Remember when I prayed, asking the angels to inhabit my dwelling, to protect and to cover me? Again, my prayers were heard because my angels were absolutely on guard. However, that night, God allowed me to watch the manifestation of my prayer unfold. And, once He showed me how He manifested what I had been praying for, I was humbled. I knew then why it was that I was led to pray for the team of civil servants that were there protecting me. God was answering my prayer. I was looking for God to answer it one way and because of that, I was missing how He had already answered it. My second little *pearl* of wisdom that I would like to offer is to look for God in the small things. He moves subtly and not explosively. And He does not have to answer you how you expect Him to. If you put Him in a box, in a box He will stay. So, if your blessing is outside of that box, you may end up missing that too. In my prayer, I asked God to protect me from dangers seen and unseen. I did not tell Him how to do it or ask Him how He was going to do it. I just prayed that He would. And, when I *saw* complete strangers who put my safety ahead of my own, my heart was full.

I was humbled. Humbled before a God that answers simple routine prayers. God is just faithful like that; even when I was not always.

Sometimes we overlook the faithfulness of God because we get so accustomed to receiving, and things just working out in our favor. Not thanking the One who is working things out. If it were not for that noise at my front door, I would have continued to miss the little *pearls* of God's faithfulness that the Holy Spirit was trying to enlighten me with. True, civil servants came out to protect and cover me that night, but God is the Master Servant. True, the angels keep and shield me, but they are at God's command. He is Lord over everything. So, the last little *pearl* of wisdom that I can share from this little experience is that even when we are not, God is faithful. He is faithful in providing for me. He is faithful in keeping me. He is faithful in protecting me. And His angels were my hedge of covering that night. I am thankful for the methods He chooses to use to keep me, and even those, that He places in my path, on assignment, to protect me.

#TeamGodDoesListen

11

Why Doubt? God Is *Always* On It...

For He says, "At the acceptable time (the time of grace), I listened to you. And I helped you on the Day of Salvation." Behold, now is the 'acceptable time.' Behold, now is the Day of Salvation...2 Corinthians 6:2

Compassion...

Reference scripture: John 5:2-10 states, "Now in Jerusalem, near the Sheep Gate, there is a pool, which is called in Hebrew Bethesda, having five colonnades. In these colonnades lay a great number of people who were sick, blind, lame, withered, [waiting for the stirring of the water; for an angel of the Lord went down into the pool at appointed seasons and stirred up the water; the first one to go in after the water was stirred was healed of his disease]. There was a certain man there who had been paralyzed for thirty-eight years. When Jesus noticed him lying there [helpless], knowing that he had been in that condition a long time, He said to him, 'Do you want to get well?' The invalid (i.e., disabled) answered, 'Sir, I have no one to put me in the pool when the water is stirred up, and while I am coming [to get into it myself], someone else steps down ahead of me.' Jesus said to him, 'Get up; pick up your mat and walk.' Immediately the man was healed and recovered his strength and picked up his mat and walked." Now, I am sure that many of you have heard this parable, at least, once. And maybe like myself, you have a pre-conceived revelation of what you *think* you are about to receive. On that note, my first little *pearl* of wisdom is: "Stay empty and open, ready to receive when reading God's Word. Once you close off your mind from getting anything 'new' or 'fresh,' you won't. Because God's Word is *ever*-living, we should be posturing ourselves to be *ever*-learning. Expecting to get something 'new' every time we read it." Now, back to our regularly scheduled program. It was not until I did what I am asking you to do that I received something different. And the Holy Spirit gave me a different perspective and insight on something that had become 'common.' If you will allow me, I would like to pass on more little *pearls* of wisdom that were shared with me.

My second little *pearl* of wisdom that I would like to share is regarding placement; God's placement. God will place you exactly where you need to be, in order to receive exactly what He has for you. This *dis*-abled man could have been placed anywhere, or by any other of the colonnades. However,

Why Doubt? God Is Always On It...

his placement was methodical. He was right where he needed to be, in the path that he needed to be in, in order to have his encounter with Jesus. Have you ever had an encounter with Jesus? Do you remember where you were? It is at these 'encounter' points that *everything* changes. Because this *dis*-abled man was in direct alignment of where he was supposed to be, further confirms that God is Omniscient (i.e., all-knowing). You may not think that God knows where you are, but He does. If He knows the hairs which are numbered on your head (Luke 12:7), then you have to know that He knows exactly where you are; even if you have not said a word *or* if you are trying to hide. We are always on God's radar. So, do not ever think that you are too far gone, that God cannot come and get you. Psalm 139:1-13 says it best, "O Lord, You have examined my heart and know everything about me. You know when I sit down or stand up. You know my thoughts even when I am far away. You see me when I travel and when I rest at home. You know everything I do. You know what I am going to say even before I say it, Lord. You go before me and follow me. You place your hand of blessing on my head. Such knowledge is too wonderful for me, too great for me to understand! I can never escape from Your Spirit! I can never get away from Your presence! If I go up to heaven, You are there; if I go down to the grave, You are there. If I ride the wings of the morning, if I dwell by the farthest oceans, even there Your hand will guide me, and Your strength will support me. I could ask the darkness to hide me and the light around me to become night — but even in darkness I cannot hide from You." I know that was a little lengthy, but isn't God's Word good?

With God being so strategic, this encounter was no accident. While all the other infirmed people were waiting for the angel to 'trouble' the water, they were not prepared for what was about to happen next. Jesus is so radical that when He steps onto *any* scene, He shows that He does not have to follow *any* protocol. He *is* protocol. He can do whatever He wants to do, for whomever He wants, however he wants to do it. PERIOD. So, my next little *pearl* of wisdom is to not always look for God to do things in your life the way He may do things in the next person's life. God is not a copycat God. He can do for you something that has never been done before. That is why you cannot compare your blessings to your neighbor's. So, put some respect on His name and begin expecting Him to manifest an out-of-this-world blessing!

As I began dissecting this Word a little deeper, the Holy Spirit began showing me different insights. The encounter between Jesus and this *dis*-abled man occurred in Jerusalem. Jerusalem is known as the holy city of peace, the city of David, or Zion. Location. Location. Location. I am telling you. God is

Why Doubt? God Is Always On It...

so strategic! From the significance of which city, the miracle occurred in, to the name of the pool where the *dis*-abled man was placed, to the timing of the miracle, there is purpose for God's plan and every piece involved. Again, I say to just trust Him because He knows what He is doing. And, wherever He places you, stay there until He tells you to move.

With God, every piece to this puzzle has significance. For instance, the name of one of the pools, where the infirmed gathered, was called Bethesda. Now, Bethesda has a dual meaning; depending on how you look at it and which angle you are looking at it from. If you are the one *needing* to be healed, then it means 'house of mercy' or the 'house of grace.' However, the oxymoron is that it was also known as the 'house of disgrace,' because of the unpleasant sight of all the infirmed who gathered there. The porch also has significance because biblically speaking, the number 5 represents God's benevolence, compassion, or grace. Let me ask you a question, "Have you ever been comfortable some place where it *should've* been uncomfortable?" Some of the reasons why a person may become complacent may be because they do not have any more fight left in them. They may somehow think that they deserved whatever the outcome was. Or, a person may not have the confidence, or faith, that the situation could ever change. As I looked at this *dis*-abled man's life, I wondered if he ever got tired of the same old routine, with no change in sight? I wondered if he ever wanted to give up or quit? Or he just got sick and tired from being sick and tired? Tired of having to be carried around? Tired from always having to depend on people? Tired from the attitudes of the people he had to depend on? Tired from not being able to do anything for himself like he wanted to? Tired from looking down at his legs that were, in his eyes, present, but completely useless? This useless 'baggage' of his legs, he had been carrying around for years had yet to serve him any purpose. What was the point? Psst...Do not forget God's promise, "Nothing that you have will be wasted. It may not look like it is useful now, but it will not be wasted. It may even be old or out-of-date, but it will not be wasted. It may not look like what other folks have, but it will not be wasted. Nothing that God has given you will be wasted. Nothing that God has taken you through will be wasted." Always hold onto that.

With all the strikes seemingly against this *disabled* man, "What would keep a man like him going? A man with so *many* visible infirmities. A man who clearly has not beaten the odds. A man who himself, become a left-over. A man who was probably a disgrace to many. A man who may even be an embarrassment, or has brought shame, upon his family." FYI: Do not ever be too quick to judge a person by their condition, or state that you meet them in. The

Why Doubt? God Is Always On It...

same grace that you received while you were in your condition, is the same grace that they will need in order to get through theirs. So, pass it on...

As I meditated on this man and the attitude he had to maintain, I wondered what it was that pushed him to get up another day and start his process all over again? What made him think, or believe, that maybe today would be different from yesterday, versus all the other days? Of course, I do not have the answers, but what I do know is that after thirty-eight long years of doing the same old thing, getting the same old results, some folks would call that lunacy. Doing the same thing but expecting something different. But, if I could be given the grace to produce my own speculations, I would like to think that sometimes lunacy (i.e., being a *little* bit crazy) can be a good thing. You have to be a *little* bit crazy doing the same thing, the same way for so long; yet, expecting different results. You have to be a *little* bit crazy to be in a situation for so long, with the looks of no hope in sight, yet you keep going. You have to be a *little* bit crazy to live your life stepping out on faith, from your comfort zone into the uncomfortable where your dependence is on other people. Yes, you have to be a *little* bit crazy to show up, every day, to be put on public display, revealing your frailties, infirmities, and vulnerabilities, to all who walk by. Yes, I would say that this *dis*-abled man was a *little* bit crazy. LOL. But can I tell you what he did receive for being a *little* bit crazy? An 'All things are possible with God' kind of blessing!

In this one encounter with Jesus, this man went from being *dis*-abled, to all things being made *able* with God. But you gotta know that this man, looking crazy, showed up every day, when he did not feel like it. This man, looking crazy, showed up every day when the weather was bad. This man, looking crazy, showed up every day even if he was sick. This man, looking crazy, showed up every day, even when his friends wanted him to goof off his day. This man, looking crazy, showed up every day, regardless of how things looked like they were not changing. This man, looking crazy, by showing up every day, put him in a position to receive from the Blesser Himself. Right there on the spot! How is that for lunacy? Told you a *little* bit crazy sometimes pays off. LOL.

From the evidence of this one man, another little *pearl* of wisdom to that no matter what, always keep your position. Always keep your will positioned towards God. Always keep your mind positioned on the things of God. Always keep your heart postured to receive that which God has for you. This man, although he had given excuse after excuse as to why he thought he could not be healed, *still* showed up every day. How far will you go for an 'All things are possible with God,' kind of blessing?

Another little *pearl* of wisdom that was given

Why Doubt? God Is Always On It...

to me deals with the importance of time. Time is something that none of us have control over. Time is something we cannot give nor is it something that we can take back. It does not matter what you go through in life or how long it lasts, God is the only One who can restore the years which have been lost. I do not want to lose you right here because I am about to offer you an alternative different than before, and the coin is about to be flipped. Here we go. This man, who is by the way nameless, has been in his condition for an exceptionally long time; thirty-eight years to be exact. For thirty-eight years, he had been in his mess. For thirty-eight years, he had been making excuses. For thirty-eight years, he had been waiting on someone else to do it for him. For thirty-eight years, he had gotten complacent just living in his circumstance(s). For thirty-eight years, he had made up his mind that he was willing to accept the hand that life had dealt him. Sounds to me that after thirty-eight years, he may have come close to thinking that things would never get better. That things would never change. That he would just have to live out the remaining of his life with his infirmity. The Bible does not give any back text on why, how, or what caused this man to have been lame for so long. All it does is confirm that he had been living like this for an exceptionally long time. Now, I have never been physically *dis*-abled, but I have been mentally, emotionally, and spiritually *dis*-abled. But God *is* able. Able to take a *dis*-abled man and make him *able* for His glory. "Now to Him who is able to do immeasurably more than all we ask or imagine, according to His power that is at work within us (Ephesians 3:20)." I need you to see that God's Word is living, and in it and through it, He has already accounted for everything that we need. Knowing that God has already accounted for our *dis*-ableness means that He has given us His grace to be *able* to pick up our mats and walk; just like the once *dis*-abled man in this parable. This man, being stuck in his condition, looked like he had lost so much time. But, when God heals, there is nothing you can lose that God is not able to restore. And He promises that your latter days will be greater than your former days. Deuteronomy 30:3 says, "God, your God, will restore everything you lost; He will have compassion on you." Therefore, stop allowing your own boundaries to keep you from getting off the steps.

    My next little *pearl* of wisdom is to be mindful of who and to what you are surrendering. Here is how it was explained to me. Think of a balance scale. As you put more weight on one side versus the other, the scale shifts. The more weight you add on one side, the lower the scale drops on the other side. Can you envision one side of the scale now being higher than the other? Think of this balancing scale as your flesh versus your spirit. The more you pull down the strongholds of your flesh, the higher the scale of your spirit will be able to rise. As you surrender control of your flesh (i.e., putting all the weight on the scale), you are being freed. You are being emptied. You are releasing your burdens (Matthew 11:28). You are trusting someone else to carry the load — the Holy Spirit. And, in an instant, the compassion of God can change the balancing scale of your life. You just have to believe. When the Holy Spirit showed me that demonstration of the balancing scale, He was showing me how we hold onto things, in our flesh, that ultimately weighs us down. And we may not even realize that we are even holding on. Prime example, when Jesus asked this man if he wanted to get better, initially, Jesus did not get a straight answer. This *dis*-abled man was choosing to hold onto something that was weighing him down. I am not talking about his physical *dis*-ableness, but more so, his mental, emotional, and spiritual *dis*-ableness. I would say that he was *dis*-abled in these areas as well because of how he answered when he was asked the one question that I am sure he waited his whole life to be asked, "Do you want to get well?" In this one simple question, the Holy Spirit showed me just how powerful your confession is. Just because something can change, does not mean that it will. Change your confession and watch the dynamics of things start changing around you. Life and death are in the power of your tongue (Proverbs

18:21). So, be mindful of the words you allow to speak over your atmosphere because circumstances can change. It is up to you how.

What I love about this scripture is that after Jesus heard this *dis*-abled man's excuses, He did not even acknowledge, or feed into, the responses that he had spoken. This move was such a 'Boss' move because Jesus did not entertain the excuses. Jesus did not try to console, or soothe, this man. Even though this man complained of always coming in last place. If I were a fly on the wall, I could only imagine some of the responses that Jesus could have told this man. Maybe some of the same responses that He may have wanted to tell me when I was stuck in my *dis*-ableness. He may have said something like, "Girl, get yourself up. Stop it with all of the excuses. The 'I Am' is in your presence, standing right in front of you. Do you not understand that I am here for you? Do you not understand that I will leave the ninety-nine to come back for the one — You? Do you not understand that in My presence you have the fullness of being made whole? Do you not understand that I Am life and that in My presence even death has to lie down? Death of your *dis*-ableness has to lie down. Death of your circumstances has to lie down. Death of a *dis*-abled mind-set, death of a broken heart, death of your insecurities and vulnerability, e-v-e-r-y-t-h-i-n-g has to lie down in My presence. Do you not understand who I am? I Am that which I Am. Do you not understand that My grace covers everything? Do you not understand how much I love you? Yes, 'You!' Girl, stop tripping!" Moments like these, I like to call, "Getting called to the carpet" moments. Life-altering, life-changing moments that not only show you who you are in Christ. But, even more so, it shows you who He is in you. God loves you and He sent His One and Only Son just for you; to take your place. Is that not compassion or what? Compassion for His children who would not even put Him first. Compassion for His children that He knew would turn their backs on Him. Compassion for His children who would deny Him and curse Him. Compassion for His own children who would not even believe that He is who He says He is. There is no greater love shown than compassion for one's children who do not even acknowledge God, the Father, as their own. God shows His compassion for us every day. And every day that you are a recipient of God's grace, you have to know that there is nothing that your Father in Heaven won't do for you.

#TeamYourPearlsAreNeededForTheJourney

12

Just Because You *Can*, Doesn't Mean You *Should*...

Those who live according to the flesh have their minds set on what the flesh desires; but those who live in accordance with the Spirit have their minds set on what the Spirit desires. The mind governed by the flesh is death, but the mind governed by the Spirit is life and peace...Romans 8:5-7

Self-control...

As I *God*-vigate my journey, a valuable lesson that I learned early on, is that just because something is possible, does not make it permissible. Just because you *can* jump off a bridge, does it mean you should? Just because you bought a dozen Krispy Kreme donuts, while the 'hot' light was on, does that mean that you should eat them all? Or just because you *want* that Louis Vuitton bag, does it mean that it is in your budget right now to buy it? Knowing that your rent and car note is due the following week? Every single one of these choices are possible. But just

Just Because You Can, Doesn't Mean You Should...

because you can do something, should you? With every choice, there is a consequence. If you always yield to satisfying your desires, without thinking about the consequences, what are your actions saying? If you buy your wants and beg your needs, what are your actions saying? True, you may get temporary fulfillment from a permanent decision, but what happens later? Can you deal with the repercussions of that permanent decision? Life is all about choices. And the timing of those choices is paramount. Let me give you an example. Remember, this is a judge-free zone.

Being raised by a single mother, there were times when, in my mind, it looked like I was going without. I mean, I had the things that I needed, but I just did not always have the things that I wanted. And, as a child, having what you want kind of supersedes your needs. So, my remedy to help compensate for what I believed to be a 'disadvantage,' was to get my wants on my own; by myself. So yes. This beautiful and innocent little face that you see, was once a thief! Hard to believe, huh? And do you want to know something crazy? The people that I would steal with somehow convinced me that it would *be* my innocent little face that would keep me from getting caught and suffering any *real* consequences. See how peer pressure can pump you up? Again, judgment-free zone. First, let me say that stealing anything once, is one time too many. And I do not condone my actions. I knew better, but I did not do better. I have repented and God has forgiven me. And the only reason I am sharing this story is so that someone else may see that for every action, there is a consequence; good or bad. And, before you make *any* choice, think about the possible repercussions. And, if you need to practice some restraint, or self-control, do so because your choices do not just affect you. Now, back to my thieving little self. I may have been around 10 or 11-years-old when I mustered up the courage to start my *bandit*-ism antics. Initially, my conquests were 'little' things. For instance, 'little' things like taking coins out of my grandmother's purse or taking a few dollars bills out of my grandfather's wallet. At the time, I was too young to realize that by taking 'little' things, which would lead to me taking 'larger' things that I was not ready to handle. 'Larger' things that would ultimately take a longer time to repair the damaged relationship that I sabotaged with my actions. I am talking about the time it took to rebuild the trust that I would betray. Nevertheless, I stole anyway. I was a child, with child-like tendencies; thinking I was invincible or too smart to ever get caught. Stealing became like an addiction for me because the more I was able to get away with, the more I wanted to do it. And the initial fear that I had was diminishing further and further away after every feat. Stealing was becoming easy. So easy that it became frightening. And each time, I promised that if I got away with it, that this would be my last time.

Just Because You Can, Doesn't Mean You Should…

Wrong. The only thing that 'getting with it' did, was give me a false confidence that I was now ready for the 'big league.' And ya' girl started stealing from almost any store that I went into. I remember telling myself that I would never do it again. But, yet again, I was getting addicted to that high of getting away with it. And, seemed like the opportunity was always there. And it did not help that I did not *look* the part. I looked like an innocent little catholic school kid. I actually *was* a little catholic school kid, but just one who was getting out of control and lacked any self-control! The more stuff that I was able to accumulate, the more my mind convinced me that I was unstoppable. That is, until I almost got caught and I had to slow my roll. I remember this like it was yesterday. I remember me and an accomplice were in this one store. They went their way, and I went my way, and we were doing 'our' thing. One of the security guards began walking behind me, following me around. After a few seconds, I decided to just leave. So, I headed for the entrance. But this guy continued to walk behind me. I knew for sure that I was caught. However, I did not miss a beat. And, because I can keep my composure under pressure, I kept calmly walking out the sliding door of the store like I had not done anything wrong. As I was walking through the entrance doors, the security guard looked over his right shoulder and saw the accomplice that I had come into the store with, in line paying for their items. He stopped dead in

Little Pearls of Wisdom...The Grace Chronicles

his tracks. They locked eyes. And then, he slowly turned around and started to walk back inside the store. I did not really understand the totality of what was happening; the caution lights blinking. The warning signs that I should have read. Or basically, the second chance that I was being given of God's hand of grace covering me. Was I going to continue stealing because I had gotten away with it so many times before? And the rush of getting away with it this last time was exhilarating. Was I always going to have an accomplice there to use as a decoy when the urge to steal came upon me? Or was I going to hang up my 'stealing hat' at such a ripe old age of 10 or 11 years old? That split second moment was my inflection point. Because it was at that moment that I knew that I was being given a choice to make. The choice was not going to be made for me, but I was being given the opportunity to make it myself. This choice was going to determine which door I would choose. A choice in which would determine if I took the path to the left or to the right. A choice in which was going to determine the trajectory of my life. A choice of whether or not life or death would be in my future. Well, if you had not already guessed it, I took learning from my inflection point for $300 Alex. That last encounter was a little too close for comfort for me. That last encounter scared me straight because it was this last encounter that changed my mind-set.

From this little excursion of mine alone, there

Just Because You Can, Doesn't Mean You Should...

were a few little *pearls* of wisdom that I walked away with. Oh yeah. Remember when I mentioned that it had taken me longer to rebuild what I had torn down? Well, I did not mention what bridge it was that I had torn down. It was the one between my grandmother and me. I would not say that I tore it down, because of the forgiving woman that she was. But I sure made it wobbly! Having to look at her face, filled with disappointment, from my lack of self-control, made me feel almost invisible. Like dirt or the gum on the bottom of your shoe. But my grandmother, being the strong woman of God that she was, you want to know what she did when she found me stealing out of her purse one time? Because you know just because I was stealing from the stores did not mean that I had stopped my dibbling and dabbling at home, right? Anyway, can you believe that this woman told me that I could keep what I had stolen from her? Which leads me to my first little *pearl* of wisdom that my grandmother was trying to teach me centered around integrity. Without integrity, a man does not have anything. And the only way that you can stand in integrity is if you are disciplined and practice self-control. Hence, the word self-control, which means that the responsibility is totally on yours. This was all on me baby girl. Therefore, I could not blame anyone else for my choices. Always remember that choices have consequences. I had to stand accountable in my truth, even though I did not want to.

Little Pearls of Wisdom...The Grace Chronicles

Outside of the hurt I could see on her face, she told me, "Since you wanted something bad enough to where you felt the need to steal it from me, keep it." I was so ashamed and embarrassed I think I hid under the bed just crying because I hurt my 'Calgon' queen, and she was the last person I would have never wanted to hurt. I did not need any more security guards or interventions. I was done! Although she had forgiven me, it took a long time for me to forgive myself. The second little *pearl* of wisdom that she was trying to teach me is to never compromise my character, or worth, going after acquiring the 'tangibles' of life. There is more to you than 'stuff.' Do not let that validate you. That is not where your worth comes from. All the 'stuff' in the world did not compare to the feeling of shame and embarrassment I suffered from my actions. And not to mention, putting in jeopardy the bond of trust that I had from the one person in the world that gave me the shoes off her feet.

I believe the last little *pearl* of wisdom that my grandmother was she was trying to instill in me was, "Just because you have access to something does not mean that you can take it. Possible does not always mean permissible." God, using my grandmother's strong and powerful sermon, along with the security guard who literally turned the other cheek, gave me a whole different outlook on what it means to deny the flesh. And, just how important it is to do it every

Just Because You Can, Doesn't Mean You Should...

single day! I may be a whole lot of other things, but a thief, I am no longer! To God be the glory for His grace in giving me more chances than I deserve.

Having experienced some of the lows that I have been through in my life has had its pros and cons. It has been two-fold. Two-fold because even though I was not proud of some of the decisions that I had made, without making them, I do not know if I would have gathered the little *pearls* of wisdom that have become essential as I continue my journey. So, in hindsight, you must know that God knows what He is doing. God knew what it would take to get me to where I am now. God knew what it would take for me to walk in the assignment that He purposed for my life. God also knew that everything that I have been through would not be wasted. It would be the platform for my testimony. It would be the platform for me sharing Him with others. God knew that this platform would be the open opportunity for me to introduce Him to others. The only reason that I am not ashamed to share my story with you is because it lets you know that a perfect God loves an imperfect Me. An imperfect Me that God has forgiven. An imperfect Me that God says He can *still* use. An imperfect Me that God *still* wants. An imperfect Me that God *still* allows His grace and mercy to cover me as I *God*-vigate on my journey. Yes, a perfect God loves an imperfect you as well...

#TeamPerfectlyFlawedAndStillLoved

13

Out Of The Ashes I Rise...

To all who mourn in Israel, He will give a crown of beauty for ashes, a joyous blessing instead of mourning, festive praise instead of despair. In their righteousness, they will be like great oaks that the Lord has planted for His own glory...
Isaiah 61:3

It always amazes me the illustrations the Holy Spirit shows me relating to the practicalities of my life. God's timing is *always* right-on-time. Let me share this. It was a few days after, what would have been my 18th wedding anniversary, when something *very* unusual happened. It was unusual because if I am being transparent, after maybe the first year of being separated from my husband, the 'date' that used to be significant, had slowly begun to dissipate like the puffballs of a dandelion flower. I know that description just sounded so whimsical and free, but in all seriousness, my marriage had been slain. Slain, in the sense, that the emotions that were once there, were now unconscious. Slain, in the sense, that there was no mental nor any emotional support being shared between us. There was also no spiritual nor physical support being exchanged as well. That may sound a little blunt and harsh, but that's transparency. So now, after being separated going on three years, my life was drastically changing. So drastic that four, yes f-o-u-r, books were birthed out of me that I had no idea with which I was even pregnant. And, to my surprise, not only were they all written and published in 2020, but they were all about my life and my experiences. And not necessarily the glorified version of myself that most of us like to present. This was the good, the bad, and the very ugly put-on-display, version of myself. I did not understand as I was going through it, but I better understand the process now as to why things had to happen how they did. I had to go through a gruesome, but necessary, season of exposure, transparency, healing, and restoration. In order to embrace the person that I was becoming, I had to memorialize the person that I once was. Thereby, being fully prepared, and equipped, to evolve into the woman that God says that I am.

Now, with that being said, while driving into work one morning, the word *widow* kept ringing in my spirit. According to what I believed the meaning of what a widow was, I clearly did not know why, or even understand, why this word kept whispering in my ear. The more I heard it though, the more anxious

Little Pearls of Wisdom...The Grace Chronicles

I became. Anxious because I knew that the Holy Spirit was trying to impart more perspective, or insight, into something. But what? So, I began praying and meditating on this one little word — widow. Now, according to the most common definition, a widow is defined as a woman who has lost her spouse, or partner, by death; and usually has not remarried. We all know that, right? Although I was given a second, unfamiliar definition that I still was not understanding. The alternate definition of a widow is a woman whose spouse, or partner, leaves her alone, or ignores her frequently, or for prolonged periods of time, to engage in a usually specified activity. It was not until I meditated on both of these definitions that I was given a third definition. However, this definition was not found in the dictionary, like the previous two definitions. This definition that I was given, was a spiritual definition told to me by the Holy Spirit. My goal is to give it to you exactly how it was given to me. So, here it goes. For the sake of this illustration, a widow was *not* gender specific. And the spiritual definition that I was given of what a widow was, was *anyone* who has ever been in any type of intimate, or covenant, relationship with another, that has been disrupted, broken, or severed. And, when a relationship between two people comes to an abrupt halt, you enter a state of *widow*-dom; so, to say. Now, it does not matter if the severed relationship was with a spouse, a child, or a loved one. You have to give that relationship the appropriate time to grieve because grieving *is* absolutely necessary. Grieving is sometimes hard to accept but is a necessary part of the process of healing. My advice to you is to process this stage however you need to; just process it. There is no right or wrong answer on how to do this. Just give yourself time to acknowledge what has happened and process it, your way. It is all right if you have to take baby steps. Grief is not a stage that you have to conquer through with leaps and bounds. Just take your time and work through it. Pray through it. And know that you will get through it. This is important, so do not negate the process. You can do this! If not, you do not put yourself in a safe position. Without having the proper opportunity to grieve, a person can feel like they cannot recover from all the wind being knocked out of them. Without having the proper opportunity to grieve, a person can withdraw from the activities that they at one time loved. Without having the proper opportunity to grieve, a person can turn to other resources, just trying to fill the 'hole' or the 'void' that they now have in their life. Without having the proper opportunity to grieve, a person can end up concluding that life is just not worth living anymore. I did not realize that this was me! I think I had been holding my breath this whole time, not really processing all that I had been through. But I knew I needed to grieve what was, so that I would be able to go forward with what shall. This was something that I did not know I needed to do. And I understand now why I was prompted to share this. So, the next woman will know that it is okay to grieve. However, getting back to my morning drive, I was beginning to understand the magnitude of what it meant when I heard the word, 'widow.' And, it was beginning to have more meaning than I had originally fathomed. Being widowed had nothing to do with a physical death or anything like that. This was a spiritual death. I, myself, was a widow because a relationship that I once was intimately and covenantly tied to, had been severed. And I needed the space and room to be able to process and grieve the outcome of the season that I was in. What was a little ironic, was when I began my 12-step program. These are the same steps that are given in AA/NA meetings. Remember when I shared that I love watching 'mush' tv? Well, one of the programs I enjoy watching is called Mom. The premise of the story is about recovering addicts going through this 12-step program. When the Holy Spirit led me to delve deeper, I realized that these were the same steps that I was needing to go through, some more than others, to help me process the grief of my *widow*-dom. Here are the 12-steps:

1) **Honesty:** Admit that you are not in control and that things have begun to spin out of control
2) **Hope:** There is a Sovereign Power who is in the business of deliverance, healing, and restoration
3) **Surrender:** Make an intentional decision to submit your will and your way over to the loving care of God
4) **Courage:** You must be willing to do the hard work of standing exposed in the accountability of your choices, as well as your truth
5) **Integrity:** Never be intimidated, or ashamed, to admit to God, yourself, and to others, your wrong-doings
6) **Willingness:** Once you admit and accept the accountability of your actions, release any guilt and shame, and keep moving forward
7) **Humility:** Being an *im*-perfect human yields us the opportunity to always have to rely on a perfect God
8) **Love:** This may be one of the hardest steps you will encounter, because not only do you have to confront your actions head on, but you also have to be willing to make amends with those in whom your actions may have hurt

9) **Responsibility:** This step is on-going because the ultimate outcome is not necessarily up to you. Even though you're trying to be accountable and responsible for your choices, doesn't mean that the ones you've hurt will be as quickly forth-coming and forgiving. Don't lose hope and definitely, don't rush this step.
10) **Discipline:** This step is also on-going because in order to continue going, and growing, forward, you must be intentional, and not intimidated, to admit and correct your wrongs
11) **Awareness:** Sought through the awakening of your spirit man through reading, praying, and meditating on God's Word
12) **Service:** This is our purpose --- to be humble servants unto one another! Don't let what you've been through be wasted. Your choices, your decisions, your mistakes --- none should be wasted! Someone needs to hear your *real* testimony. It is your responsibility, and God's decree, to strengthen the one behind you (Luke 22:32); for His glory!

These 12-steps, and the process of going through them, would help lead to my healing as well. Healing leads to restoration. Restoration leads to walking a life of recovery. And, it is in this walk, as you are healing, that you reach back, lift up, and strengthen those around you. Your recovery is not just about you. Your recovery is evidence. Evidence that God is God. Evidence that God can use the messiest of situations, turn them around, all for His glory. Evidence that it does not matter where you start, it is about how you finish. Evidence that God can use the 'misfits' for His purpose. Evidence that God is a God of love, mercy, forgiveness, and compassion. Evidence that it does not matter how others see you, or how even you may see yourself, what God says about you is all that matters. And, He says that you are fearfully and wonderfully made (Psalm 139:14). God gave me another chance to evolve into the 'Me' that I know I can be. And I am not wasting this opportunity this time around!

After the Holy Spirit illuminated the insight behind the word 'widow,' I realized that my 'living' did not have to end. It did not matter what I had been through, nevertheless, I am still living. It did not matter who was not walking with me, nevertheless, I am still living. It did not matter who was for me or against me, nevertheless, I am still choosing to live. Whatever I confronted, I had to have a 'nevertheless, I'm still living' attitude. What the world says about me and what God says about me are two totally different things. The world, naturally, says that when you are considered a widow, all that is seen is that you are in a season of losing. Duly noted. You have certainly lost someone, or something,

Little Pearls of Wisdom...The Grace Chronicles

of irrevocable value. I am not belittling or dismissing that at all. We have all been in a position of 'losing,' so to say. But, for me, what I believed to be one the worst seasons of my life turned out to be something that propelled me into a purpose that I could have never imagined. From this, I *know* that I was being given grace to begin again. God's way. And it is only because of the grace of God that He allowed me to come out with some little *pearls* of wisdom for the rest of my journey. Every day I was able to walk through the season I was living in, became my testimony. My testimony in knowing that it does not matter how things look. It does not matter how things appear. It does not even matter how things may pan out. I was constantly reminded that I am blessed! I am blessed if I am married. I am blessed if I am single. I am blessed if I am separated. I am blessed even if I am divorced. I am still blessed if I am widowed. I am blessed in my infertility. I am blessed if I adopt kids. I am blessed if I have hypertension. I am blessed if I am healthy. I am blessed if I have a job. I am blessed if I do not have a job. I am blessed if I am lonely. I am blessed if I do not have a dime to my name. I am just blessed. I am blessed coming in, I am blessed going out. Wherever I go and whatever I do, God says that I am blessed (Deuteronomy 28:6)! That is why you cannot always focus on where you are because things can change. Ephesians 1:3, "Blessed be the God and Father of our Lord Jesus Christ, who hath blessed us with all spiritual blessings in heavenly places in Christ." Therefore, let me say it again, "I am blessed! You are blessed! We are blessed!"

This *widow* contemplation that I had, became my 'lightbulb moment.' It was an 'awakening' for me. An 'awakening' in my faith. An 'awakening' in my walk. An 'awakening' in my purpose. In order for something to be 'awakened,' that must mean that it was sleeping. The 'old' me, I guess you can say, was sleeping on the things of God. Sleeping on the ways of God. Sleeping on the purpose that God has for me. Sleeping on my destiny. And something had to be awakened in order for it to be able to live. Being able to grow from being a widow meant that I had been given another opportunity to move, live, and have my being in Him which gives me His undeserving grace. Grace to love in the way that God loves us. Grace to give of myself in a whole new way. Grace to allow God to order my steps. Grace to walk by faith as I *God*-vigate. Grace to fulfill God's purpose for my life. So, in my *widow*-ship, I thank God that I do not look like what I have been through. I thank God that I have not been broken beyond repair. I thank God that He breathed life into my dry bones. And I thank God that He gives me His grace as I continue my journey.

I am learning that no matter what I go through, God's grace was, is, will *always* be sufficient. I am learning that even in the breaking, God does it gracefully. Every little *pearl* of wisdom that I have gathered along the way encourages me to keep moving forward. Keep moving forward because there is more work that God wants to do to me. Keep moving forward because there is more that God wants to accomplish through me. Keep moving forward because there is more that God wants to use me for, to be a blessing to His people.

Before closing, I would like to offer my last little *pearl* of wisdom: God is a God of the 'big' picture. Sometimes you have to turn the telescope around and look at life from the opposite end. When you look at life from the wider end of the lens, it makes whatever you are looking at, a whole lot smaller. That is the whole intention. Instead of looking at what you are facing as being too big, turn the lens around. Doing this helps me to realize that my issue is a lot smaller than what I am making it out to be. I would much rather look at how 'Big' my God is rather than looking at how big my situation is. It is a simple matter of perception. So, just turn it around! Once I did, I was able to embrace a different perspective. The wider lens showed me the grace of God. And how I was given the grace to gain. The grace to gain a different mind-set. A mind-set which showed me how God can still bring good out of an unpleasant situation. The bad is only a season. It is not a lifestyle. So, do not get stuck there. Yes, you may be down. But you are not out. Get up! God's got you!

#TeamGodWillGiveYouGraceForTheJourney

Author's Snippet...

Flavor Like No Other...

"You are the salt of the earth. But what good is salt if it has lost its flavor? Can you make it salty again? It will be thrown out and trampled underfoot as worthless"...Matthew 5:13

The taste of salt has a little 'kick' to it. There is a boldness to it. Even when mixed with other ingredients, you are *still* able to taste its uniqueness. It is hard to drown out its richness. It is hard to mask its texture. It is especially hard to try and camouflage its flavor. It is poignant. And, when it makes its introduction, its presence is undeniable. The flavor that it brings can either stand all on its own or it can be comfortably blended with other ingredients. Salt makes a statement. A statement unlike any other. This is the same statement that we, as Christians, as Believers, as Disciples of Christ, should make. There ought not be any compromising on our flavor, or character. There ought not be any wavering of our integrity. There ought not be any bending of our morals or what we stand for. There ought not be any teetering of our principles, or boldness in Christ. Yet here we are, because sometimes there is. And I am pointing the finger at 'Me' first, as always. Matthew 5:13

reads, "Let me tell you why you are here. You are here to be salt-seasoning that brings out the God-flavors of this earth. If you lose your saltiness, how will people taste godliness? You have lost your usefulness and will end up in the garbage." I have read, and heard, this scripture repeatedly. However, it was not until the Holy Spirit imparted insight and gave me a different perspective about this one little word — salt. Since we all know what 'salt' is, I am going to jump right into the insight the Holy Spirit gave me. However, before I share with you what was shared with me, I would like to offer you its scientific relevance first.

    Salt, also referred to as table salt or sodium chloride, is a mineral composed of sodium and chloride ions. It basically comes from two sources: sea water and rock salt (i.e., sodium chloride mineral halite). Rock salt is formed from the evaporation of minerals that have dried up, predominantly from lakes, playas, or seas. As far as history wise, salt has been around since the beginning of time. Salt is a necessity of life; in that all life has evolved to depend on its chemical properties in order to survive. Whether it be to help and maintain fluid balance or to assist with muscle and nerve function, salt is essential. It is essential for flavoring, preservation, and even disinfecting for common household use. In conjunction to all of its functions, salt is also used medicinally. Some of us may even ingest it a couple of times a day; since it is in

Flavor Like No Other...

many of the foods we eat. Being a scientist by trade, I am fully aware of how salt is an integral ingredient to many components. However, its use naturally is not what sparked my curiosity. It was how the scripture related to 'us' as being the salt of the earth. Here is where my journey begins.

There are numerous scriptures in the Bible in which salt is used metaphorically to symbolize permanence, loyalty, durability, usefulness, purification, and value. When the earlier scripture referenced 'us' as being the salt of the earth, I was intrigued? But what exactly does that mean? And how do I play my part? And here is what was shared with me. Going back to the different metaphorical meanings of the word 'salt' that is emphasized in the Bible, the one description that kept ringing in my spirit was the word *value*. I can remember something my grandmother used to say like I just heard it yesterday. Growing up as a young woman, she would always say, "Your presence should leave an imprint. When you are absent from a room, people ought to miss you. It should be something about 'you' that makes folks notice when you are not around. This is what makes you, *You*; like nobody else can do." In other words, you should be an *asset* wherever you go and not a *liability*. The little *pearl* of wisdom that she was trying to instill in me is that there ought to be some kind of *value* that you bring to the table that no one else can bring quite like you. There ought to be a *saltiness* that only you can add. And, when it is missing, it should be noticeable that there is something lacking. There ought to be a bold kind of flavor, or spiciness in the words, which proceeded out of your belly, that rightly divides God's truth. Truth that only comes from staying in God's Word, and not the world. John 15:19 states, "You do not belong to the world, but I have chosen you out of the world. That is why the world hates you (i.e., The world wants you to lose your *saltiness*)." The 'world' will sometimes try to 'water down,' or dissolve, God's Word, and His truth. But there is no gray area for sin. Sin is sin. Period. If you listen to the lies of the devil, he will whole-heartedly try to convince you that there is always a gray area with God. And, knowing that since God is so forgiving, He *expects* you to mess up. You better not fall for the okie doke. Because the one thing you do not want to do is frustrate God's grace or take it for granted. It is not going to go well for the home team. Think about it this way. Why would the devil invest so much time and energy into deceiving you, if he did not believe the end result would be greater than if he did not stop you? Why go through all the tricks and schemes? Wasting time with all the foolery? He would not. That is why he relentlessly tries every tactic to distract you because you do have *value*. You do have something to *offer*. You do have something to *add*. You do have some flavor, God's flavor, to stir into the pot of life. Here is another little *pearl* of wisdom, "Start sprinkling. Sprinkle the salt around that God has given you. Wherever you go, leave some salt. Leave some flavor." And, when you leave, things ought to be tasting just a little bit bland. Like something is missing. Like an ingredient got overlooked. Like the seasoning needs to be tweaked just a bit. I will leave you with this — Always be ready to 'shake' things up for God and do not let anyone steal your flavor. For we, as Christians, are that missing ingredient that the world needs more of. The ingredient that opens the door for us to testify of the love, the goodness, and the grace of our God. So, get to shaking because someone may be waiting on the flavor that only you can give!

#TeamTimeToKickUpTheFlava

Words of Encouragement...

Sister(s),

You may not think that your little pearls of wisdom are particularly important or substantial right now. But trust me, they are more valuable and priceless than anything that you will ever acquire. There is nothing that can replace the lessons you have, and will learn, as you God-vigate through life. For it is these little pearls of wisdom that adds to the adorned beauty of your crown of grace. Stay true to yourself and embrace the woman that God is evolving you into. Continue to walk in grace...

#TeamWearYourCrownOfGrace

> "You're blessed when you're content with just who you are — no more, no less. That's the moment you find yourselves proud owners of everything that can't be bought"...Matthew 5:5

www.ingramcontent.com/pod-product-compliance
Lightning Source LLC
LaVergne TN
LVHW092007090526
838202LV00001B/32